Stories *for* *the* HEART

OVER 100 STORIES TO

ENCOURAGE YOUR SOUL

Compiled by Alice Gray

Multnomah Books
Sisters, Oregon

This Billy Graham Evangelistic Association
special edition is published with permission
from Questar Publishers, Inc.

STORIES FOR THE HEART
© 1996 by Questar Publishers, Inc.

Published by Multnomah Books
a part of the Questar publishing family

Compiled by Alice Gray

Photograph by Stephen Simpson, FPG International

Printed in the United States of America.

International Standard Book Number: 0-913367-67-2

For information:
QUESTAR PUBLISHERS, INC.
POST OFFICE BOX 1720
SISTERS, OREGON 97759

In memory of my mother

who taught me to love stories.

My heartfelt thanks to

The staff at Multnomah Books
for their encouragement

Casandra Lindell
for unending hours of computer input and advice

Marilyn McAuley
for friendship and eleventh hour help

Friends and family
for prayer and sending me stories over the years

Al Gray
for unselfish love and tender care through all the years

Contents

Compassion

TOGETHER

Emery Nester

A man was walking in a wilderness. He became lost and was unable to find his way out. Another man met him. "Sir, I am lost, can you show me the way out of this wilderness?" "No," said the stranger, "I cannot show you the way out of the wilderness, but maybe if I walk with you, we can find it together."

The Day Philip
Joined the Group

Paul Harvey

with acknowledgement to Rev. Harry Pritchett, Jr.,
rector of All Saints Episcopal Church in Atlanta, who called
my attention to a boy named Philip.

He was 9—in a Sunday school class of 8-year-olds.
Eight-year-olds can be cruel.

The third-graders did not welcome Philip to their group. Not just because he was older. He was "different."

He suffered from Down's syndrome and its obvious manifestations: facial characteristics, slow responses, symptoms of retardation.

One Sunday after Easter the Sunday school teacher gathered some of those plastic eggs that pull apart in the middle—the kind in which some ladies' pantyhose are packaged.

The Sunday school teacher gave one of these plastic eggs to each child.

On that beautiful spring day each child was to go outdoors and discover for himself some symbol of "new life" and place that symbolic seed or leaf or whatever inside his egg.

They would then open their eggs one by one, and each youngster would explain how his find was a symbol of "new life."

So...

The youngsters gathered 'round on the appointed day and put their eggs on a table, and the teacher began to open them.

One child had found a flower.

All the children "oohed" and "aahed" at the lovely symbol of new life.

In another was a butterfly. "Beautiful," the girls said. And it's not easy for an 8-year-old to say "beautiful."

Another egg was opened to reveal a rock. Some of the

children laughed.

"That's crazy!" one said. "How's a rock supposed to be like a 'new life'?"

Immediately a little boy spoke up and said, "That's mine. I knew everybody would get flowers and leaves and butterflies and all that stuff, so I got a rock to be different."

Everyone laughed.

The teacher opened the last one, and there was nothing inside.

"That's not fair," someone said. "That's stupid," said another.

Teacher felt a tug on his shirt. It was Philip. Looking up he said, "It's mine. I did do it. It's empty. I have new life because the tomb is empty."

The class fell silent.

From that day on Philip became part of the group. They welcomed him. Whatever had made him different was never mentioned again.

Philip's family had known he would not live a long life; just too many things wrong with the tiny body. That summer, overcome with infection, Philip died.

On the day of his funeral nine 8-year-old boys and girls confronted the reality of death and marched up to the altar— not with flowers.

Nine children with their Sunday school teacher placed on the casket of their friend their gift of love—an empty egg.

A Song in the Dark

Max Lucado

On any other day, I probably wouldn't have stopped. Like the majority of people on the busy avenue, I would hardly have noticed him standing there. But the very thing on my mind was the very reason he was there, so I stopped.

I'd just spent a portion of the morning preparing a lesson out of the ninth chapter of John, the chapter that contains the story about the man blind from birth. I'd finished lunch and was returning to my office when I saw him. He was singing. An aluminum cane was in his left hand; his right hand was extended and open, awaiting donations. He was blind.

After walking past him about five steps, I stopped and mumbled something to myself about the epitome of hypocrisy and went back in his direction. I put some change in his hand. "Thank you," he said and then offered me a common Brazilian translation, "and may you have health." Ironic wish.

Once again I started on my way. Once again the morning's study of John 9 stopped me. "Jesus saw a man, blind from birth." I paused and pondered. If Jesus were here he would see this man. I wasn't sure what that meant. But I was sure I hadn't done it. So I turned around again.

As if the giving of a donation entitled me to do so, I stopped beside a nearby car and observed. I challenged myself to see him. I would stay here until I saw more than a sightless indigent on a busy thoroughfare in downtown Rio de Janeiro.

I watched him sing. Some beggars grovel in a corner cultivating pity. Others unashamedly lay their children on blankets in the middle of the sidewalk thinking that only the hardest of hearts would ignore a dirty, naked infant asking for bread.

But this man did none of that. He stood. He stood tall. And he sang. Loudly. Even proudly. All of us had more reason to sing than he, but he was the one singing. Mainly, he sang folk songs. Once I thought he was singing a hymn, though I wasn't sure.

His husky voice was out of place amid the buzz of commerce. Like a sparrow who found his way into a noisy factory, or a lost fawn on an interstate, his singing conjured up an awkward marriage between progress and simplicity.

The passersby had various reactions. Some were curious and gazed unabashedly. Others were uncomfortable. They were quick to duck their heads or walk in a wider circle. "No reminders of harshness today, please." Most, however, hardly noticed him. Their thoughts were occupied, their agendas were full and he was...well, he was a blind beggar.

I was thankful he couldn't see the way they looked at him.

After a few minutes, I went up to him again. "Have you had any lunch?" I asked. He stopped singing. He turned his head toward the sound of my voice and directed his face somewhere past my ear. His eye sockets were empty. He said he was hungry. I went to a nearby restaurant and bought him a sandwich and something cold to drink.

When I came back he was still singing and his hands were still empty. He was grateful for the food. We sat down on a nearby bench. Between bites he told me about himself. Twenty-eight years old. Single. Living with his parents and seven brothers. "Were you born blind?"

"No, when I was young I had an accident." He didn't volunteer any details and I didn't have the gall to request them.

Though we were almost the same age, we were light-years apart. My three decades had been a summer vacation of family excursions, Sunday school, debate teams, football, and a search for the Mighty One. Growing up blind in the Third World surely offered none of these. My daily concern now involved people, thoughts, concepts, and communication. His day was stitched with concerns of survival: coins, handouts, and food. I'd go home to a nice apartment, a hot meal, and a good wife. I hated to think of the home he would encounter. I'd seen enough overcrowded huts on the hills of Rio to make a reasonable guess. And his reception...would there be anyone there to make him feel special when he got home?

I came whisker-close to asking him, "Does it make you mad that I'm not you?" "Do you ever lie awake at night wondering why the hand you were dealt was so different from the one given a million or so others born thirty years ago?"

I wore a shirt and tie and some new shoes. His shoes had holes and his coat was oversized and bulky. His pants gaped open from a rip in the knee.

And still he sang. Though a sightless, penniless hobo, he still found a song and sang it courageously. (I wondered which room in his heart that song came from.)

At worst, I figured, he sang from desperation. His song was all he had. Even when no one gave any coins, he still had his song. Yet he seemed too peaceful to be singing out of self-preservation.

Or perhaps he sang from ignorance. Maybe he didn't know what he had never had.

No, I decided the motivation that fit his demeanor was the one you'd least expect. He was singing from contentment. Somehow this eyeless pauper had discovered a candle called satisfaction and it glowed in his dark world. Someone had told him, or maybe he'd told himself, that tomorrow's joy is fathered by today's acceptance. Acceptance of what, at least for the moment, you cannot alter.

I looked up at the Niagara of faces that flowed past us. Grim. Professional. Some determined. Some disguised. But none were singing, not even silently. What if each face were a billboard that announced the true state of the owner's heart?

How many would say "Desperate! Business on the rocks!" or "Broken: In Need of Repair," or "Faithless, Frantic, and Fearful"? Quite a few.

The irony was painfully amusing. This blind man could be the most peaceful fellow on the street. No diploma, no awards, and no future—at least in the aggressive sense of the word. But I wondered how many in that urban stampede would trade their boardrooms and blue suits in a second for a chance to drink at this young man's well.

"Faith is the bird that sings while it is yet dark."

Before I helped my friend back to his position, I tried to verbalize my empathy. "Life is hard, isn't it?" A slight smile. He again turned his face toward the direction of my voice and started to respond, then paused and said, "I'd better get back to work."

For almost a block, I could hear him singing. And in my mind's eye I could still see him. But the man I now saw was a different one than the one to whom I'd given a few coins. Though the man I now saw was still sightless, he was remarkably insightful. And though I was the one with eyes, it was he who gave me a new vision.

There's Always Something Left to Love

Tony Campolo

Some years ago, I saw Lorraine Hansberry's play, *Raisin in the Sun*, and heard a passage that still haunts me. In the play, an African-American family inherits $10,000 from their father's life insurance policy. The mother of the household sees in this legacy the chance to escape the ghetto life of Harlem and move into a little house with flower boxes out in the countryside. The brilliant daughter of this family sees in the money the chance to live out her dream and go to medical school.

But the older brother has a plea that is difficult to ignore. He begs for the money so that he and his "friend" can go into business together. He tells the family that with the money he can make something of himself and make things good for the rest of them. He promises that if he can just have the money, he can give back to the family all the blessings that their hard lives have denied them.

Against her better judgment, the mother gives in to the pleas of her son. She has to admit that life's chances have never been good for him and that he deserves the chance that this money might give him.

As you might suspect, the so called "friend" skips town with the money. The desolate son has to return home and break the news to the family that their hopes for the future have been stolen and their dreams for a better life are gone. His sister lashes into him with a barrage of ugly epitaphs. She calls him every despicable thing she can imagine. Her contempt for her brother has no limits.

When she takes a breath in the midst of her tirade, the mother interrupts her and says, "I thought I taught you to love him."

Beneatha, the daughter answers, "Love him? There's nothing left to love."

And the mother responds: "There's always something left to love. And if you ain't learned that, you ain't learned nothing. Have you cried for that boy today? I don't mean for yourself and the family because we lost all that money. I mean for him: for what he's been through and what it done to him. Child, when do you think is the time to love somebody the most: when they done good and made things easy for everybody? Well then, you ain't through learning, because that ain't the time at all. It's when he's at his lowest and can't believe in himself 'cause the world done whipped him so. When you starts measuring somebody, measure him right, child, measure him right. Make sure you done taken into account what hills and valleys he done come through before he got to wherever he is."

That is grace! It is love that is given when it is not deserved. It is forgiveness given when it is not earned. It is a gift that flows like a refreshing stream to quench the fires of angry condemning words.

How much more loving and forgiving is the Father's love for us? And how much more is the grace of God for us?

Belonging

Paul Brand and Philip Yancey

John Karmegan came to me in Vellore, India, as a leprosy patient in an advanced state of the disease. We could do little for him surgically since both his feet and hands had already been damaged irreparably. We could, however, offer him a place to stay and employment in the New Life Center.

Because of one-sided facial paralysis, John could not smile normally. When he tried, the uneven distortion of his features would draw attention to his paralysis. People often responded with a gasp or a gesture of fear, so he learned not to smile. Margaret, my wife, had stitched his eyelids partly closed to protect his sight. John grew more and more paranoid about what others thought of him.

He caused terrible problems socially, perhaps in reaction to his marred appearance. He expressed his anger at the world by acting the part of a troublemaker, and I remember many tense scenes in which we had to confront John with some evidence of stealing or dishonesty. He treated fellow-patients cruelly, and resisted all authority, going so far as to organize hunger strikes against us. By almost anyone's reckoning, he was beyond rehabilitation.

Perhaps John's very irredeemability attracted my mother to him, for she often latched onto the least desirable specimens of humanity. She took to John, spent time with him, and eventually led him into the Christian faith. He was baptized in a cement tank on the grounds of the leprosarium.

Conversion, however, did not temper John's high dudgeon against the world. He gained some friends among fellow-patients, but a lifetime of rejection and mistreatment had permanently embittered him against all non-patients. One day, almost defiantly, he asked me what would happen if he visited the local Tamil church in Vellore.

I went to the leaders of the church, described John, and assured them that despite obvious deformities, he had entered a safe phase of the arrested disease and would not endanger the congregation. They agreed he could visit. "Can he take communion?" I asked, knowing that the church used a common cup. They looked at each other, thought for a moment, and agreed that he could also take communion.

Shortly thereafter I took John to the church, which met in a plain, whitewashed brick building with a corrugated iron roof. It was a tense moment for him. Those of us on the outside can hardly imagine the trauma and paranoia inside a leprosy patient who attempts for the first time to enter that kind of setting. I stood with him at the back of the church. His paralyzed face showed no reaction, but a trembling gave away his inner turmoil. I prayed silently that no church member would show the slightest hint of rejection.

As we entered during the singing of the first hymn, an Indian man toward the back half-turned and saw us. We must have made an odd couple: a white person standing next to a leprosy patient with patches of his skin in garish disarray. I held my breath.

And then it happened. The man put down his hymnal, smiled broadly, and patted the chair next to him, inviting John to join him. John could not have been more startled. Haltingly, he made shuffling half-steps to the row and took his seat. I breathed a prayer of thanks.

That one incident proved to be the turning point of John's life. Years later I visited Vellore and made a side trip to a factory that had been set up to employ disabled people. The manager wanted to show me a machine that produced tiny screws for typewriter parts. As we walked through the noisy plant, he shouted at me that he would introduce me to his prize employee, a man who had just won the parent corporation's all-India prize for the highest quality work with fewest rejects. As we arrived at his work station, the employee turned to greet us, and I saw the unmistakable crooked face of John Karmegan. He wiped the grease off his stumpy hand and grinned with the ugliest, the loveliest, most radiant smile I had ever seen. He held out for my inspection a palmful of the small precision screws that had won him the prize.

A simple gesture of acceptance may not seem like much, but for John Karmegan it proved decisive. After a lifetime of being judged on his own physical image, he had finally been welcomed on the basis of another Image. I had seen a replay of Christ's own reconciliation. His Spirit had prompted the Body on earth to adopt a new member, and at last John knew he belonged.

Really Winning

Michael Broome
Retold by Alice Gray

Every year thousands of young athletes from all over the world gather for the Special Olympics. The fanfare, the celebrities, the music, the excitement are nearly as grand as the regular Olympics. These athletes know what it means to give their best. They have trained for months and for years and want to win.

Several years ago, five handicapped finalists gathered at the starting line. Their hearts were pounding. Each wanted to win. The starter's gun discharged and the athletes exploded from their crouched positions and began running with all their heart. The crowd was on its feet shouting and cheering.

Suddenly one of the runners stumbled and fell flat on his face. He struggled but couldn't seem to get up. A moan and then a hush fell over the stadium. In the next moment, another child stopped running and reached down and helped the fallen child back up. The two of them finished the race together.

Courage

Author unknown

It was a few weeks before Christmas 1917. The beautiful snowy landscapes of Europe were blackened by war.

The trenches on one side held the Germans and on the other side the trenches were filled with Americans. It was World War I. The exchange of gunshots was intense. Separating them was a very narrow strip of no-man's-land. A young German soldier attempting to cross that no-man's-land had been shot and had become entangled in the barbed wire. He cried out in anguish, then in pain he continued to whimper.

Between the shells all the Americans in that sector could hear him scream. When one American soldier could stand it no longer, he crawled out of the American trenches and on his stomach crawled to that German soldier. When the Americans realized what he was doing they stopped firing, but the Germans continued. Then a German officer realized what the young American was doing and he ordered his men to cease firing. Now there was a weird silence across the no-man's-land. On his stomach, the American made his way to that German soldier and disentangled him. He stood up with the German in his arms, walked straight to the German trenches and placed him in the waiting arms of his comrades. Having done so, he turned and started back to the American trenches.

Suddenly there was a hand on his shoulder that spun him around. There stood a German officer who had won the Iron Cross, the highest German honor for bravery. He jerked it from his own uniform and placed it on the American, who walked back to the American trenches. When he was safely in the trenches, they resumed the insanity of war!

Humpty Dumpty Revisited

Vic Pentz

Humpty Dumpty sat on the wall.
Humpty Dumpty had a great fall.
All the King's horses and all the King's men
Couldn't put Humpty together again.

But soon the King himself heard of Humpty's fate. And he was deeply disturbed. So, setting aside his royal finery, disguised as a common peasant, the King slipped unnoticed through the majestic palace gates and into the rough-and-tumble street life of his kingdom.

The King meandered through the back streets and alleys in search of Humpty. After several days and nights the persistent monarch found him. Humpty's shattered body was scattered over a ten-foot circle amidst the broken glass and flattened beer cans of a back alley.

Though weak from his searching, the King was overjoyed at the sight of Humpty. He ran to his side and cried, "Humpty! It is I—your King! I have powers greater than those of my horses and men who failed to put you together again. Be at peace. I am here to help!"

"Leave me alone," Humpty's mouth retorted. "I've gotten used to this new way of life. I kind of like it now."

"But—" was all the King could get out before Humpty continued.

"I tell you, I'm fine. I like it here. That trash can over there...the way the sun sparkles on the broken glass. This must be the garden spot of the world!"

The King tried again. "I assure you my kingdom has much more to offer than this back alley—there are green mountains, rolling surfs, exciting cities...."

But Humpty would hear none of it. And the saddened King returned to the palace.

A week later one of Humpty's eyes rolled skyward only to see once again the concerned face of the King standing over his fractured pieces.

"I've come to help," firmly stated the King.

"Look, leave me alone, will you?" said Humpty. "I've just seen my psychiatrist, and he assures me that I'm doing a fine job of coping with my environment as it is. You're a cop-out. A man has to deal with life as it comes. I'm a realist."

"But wouldn't you rather walk?" asked the King.

"Look," Humpty's mouth replied, "once I get up and start walking I'll have to stay up and keep walking. At this point in my life I'm not ready to make a commitment like that. So, if you'll excuse me—you're blocking my sun."

Reluctantly the King turned once again and walked through the streets of his kingdom back to the palace.

It was over a year before the King ventured to return to Humpty's side.

But, sure enough, one bright morning one of Humpty's ears perked up at the sure, steady strides of the King. This time he was ready. Humpty's eye turned toward the tall figure just as his mouth managed the words, "My King!"

Immediately the King fell to his knees on the glass-covered pavement. His strong, knowing hands gently began to piece together Humpty's fragments. After some time, his work completed, the King rose to full height, pulling up with him the figure of a strong young man.

The two walked hand in hand throughout the kingdom. Together they stood atop lush green mountains. They ran together along deserted beaches. They laughed and joked together as they strolled the gleaming cities of the King's domain. This went on forever. And to the depth, breadth, and height of their friendship there was no end.

Once while walking together down the sidewalk in one of the King's cities, Humpty overheard a remark that made his heart leap with both the joy of his new life and the bitter memory of the back alley. Someone said, "Say, who are those two men?"

Another replied, "Why the one on the left is old Humpty Dumpty. I don't know the one on the right—but they sure look like brothers!"

Lessons from a Young Nurse

Rebecca Manley Pippert

In an article in *Campus Life* a young nurse writes of her pilgrimage in learning to see in a patient the image of God beneath a very "distressing disguise."

Eileen was one of her first patients, a person who was totally helpless. "A cerebral aneurysm (broken blood vessels in the brain) had left her with no conscious control over her body," the nurse writes. As near as the doctors could tell Eileen was totally unconscious, unable to feel pain and unaware of anything going on around her. It was the job of the hospital staff to turn her every hour to prevent bedsores and to feed her twice a day "what looked like a thin mush through a stomach tube." Caring for her was a thankless task. "When it's this bad," an older student nurse told her, "you have to detach yourself emotionally from the whole situation...." As a result, more and more she came to be treated as a thing, a vegetable....

But the young student nurse decided that she could not treat this person like the others had treated her. She talked to Eileen, sang to her, encouraged her and even brought her little gifts. One day when things were especially difficult and it would have been easy for the young nurse to take out her frustrations on the patient, she was especially kind. It was Thanksgiving Day and the nurse said to the patient, "I was in a cruddy mood this morning, Eileen, because it was supposed to be my day off. But now that I'm here, I'm glad. I wouldn't have wanted to miss seeing you on Thanksgiving. Do you know this is Thanksgiving?"

Just then the telephone rang, and as the nurse turned to answer it, she looked quickly back at the patient. Suddenly, she writes, Eileen was *"looking at me … crying*. Big damp circles stained her pillow, and she was shaking all over."

That was the only human emotion that Eileen ever showed any of them, but it was enough to change the whole attitude of the hospital staff toward her. Not long afterward, Eileen died. The young nurse closes her story, saying, "I keep thinking about her.... It occurred to me that I owe her an awful lot. Except for Eileen, I might never have known what it's like to give myself to someone who can't give back."

ONE

I am only one, but I am one.
I cannot do everything, but I can do something.
What I can do, I should do and,
with the help of God, I will do!

Everett Hale

It Matters

Jeff Ostrander

Along the coast of the vast Atlantic ocean there lived an old man. Each day when the tide went out he would make his way along the beach for miles. Another man who lived not far away would occasionally watch as he vanished into the distance and later notice that he had returned. The neighbor also noticed that, as he walked, the old man would often stoop down to lift something from the sand and then toss it away into the water.

One day, when the old man went down to the beach this neighbor followed to satisfy his curiosity and, sure enough, as he watched, the old man bent down and gently lifted something from the sand and threw it into the ocean. By the time the old man made his next stop the neighbor had come near enough to see that he was picking up a starfish which had been stranded by the retreating tide and would, of course, die of dehydration before the tide returned. As the old man turned to return it to the ocean the neighbor called out with a degree of mockery in his voice, "Hey, old timer! What are you doing? This beach goes on for hundreds of miles, and thousands of starfish get washed up every day! Surely you don't think that throwing a few back is going to matter."

The old man listened and paused for a moment, then held the starfish in his hand out toward his neighbor. "It matters to this one."

Understanding Mercy

Alice Gray

There was a young man in Napoleon's army who committed a deed so terrible that it was worthy of death. The day before he was scheduled for the firing squad, the young man's mother went to Napoleon and pleaded for mercy for her son.

Napoleon replied, "Woman, your son does not deserve mercy."

"I know," she answered. "If he deserved it then it would not be mercy."

TOO WONDERFUL

"Some of God's attributes are too wonderful to understand.
But even if they remain darkness to the intellect,
let them be sunshine for your soul."

Author unknown

Encouragement

CHOSEN

Marie Curling

Whenever I'm disappointed with my lot in life, I stop and think about little Jamie Scott. Jamie was trying out for a part in his school play. His mother told me that he'd set his heart on being in it, though she feared he would not be chosen. On the day the parts were awarded, I went with her to collect him after school. Jamie rushed up to her, eyes shining with pride and excitement. "Guess what, Mum," he shouted, and then said those words that remain a lesson to me: "I've been chosen to clap and cheer."

The First Robin

William E. Barton
(*Unusual typesetting from original text*)

Now the Winter had been Long, and Very Cold, and the Snow had been deep, and Spring had not yet come. And I rose early in the morning, and I looked out of mine Window, and Behold a Robin.

And I called unto Keturah, and said, Come quickly, and see thou hasten thine arrival at the Window. For here is a Friend of ours that is Come from a Far Country to Visit us.

And Keturah came to the Window, and she also beheld the Robin.

Now the Robin looked at us, and hopped about upon the Cold and Bare Ground, and looked for the Early Worm, but the Bird was Earlier than the Worm. And Keturah went to her Kitchen to see what she might find that the Robin would eat.

And I spake to the Robin, and said:

Behold thou hast been where it was Warm, and the Sun did Shine. And thou couldest have stayed there. But here thou art. And thou comest while it is yet Winter, for the Prophecy of Spring is in thy Blood. Thy faith is the substance of things hoped for and the evidence of things not seen. Thou hast come many miles, yea hundreds of miles, to a land that lies desolate, because thou hast within thy soul the assurance that Spring is near. Oh, that there were in human life some assurance that would send folk forth to their High Destiny with as compelling a Conviction!

And I thought of the Eye, that it is formed in darkness, but formed for the light; and the Ear that is wondrously shaped in Silence, but made for the hearing of Musick; and of the Human Soul that is born into a world where Sin is, yet born with the hope of Righteousness.

And I blessed the Little Bird that had caused me to think

of these things.

And I went forth into town that day, and people said, Safed. Behold is it not a cold and long Winter?

And I said, Speak to me no more of Winter.

And they said, Wherefore should we not speak of Winter? Behold the Thermometer and the Empty Coal Bin.

But I held mine Head Proudly and I said:

Speak to me not of Winter. Behold, on this morning I did see the First Robin. For me henceforth it is Spring.

Don't Quit

Charles R. Swindoll

Ignace Jan Paderewski, the famous composer-pianist, was scheduled to perform at a great concert hall in America. It was an evening to remember—black tuxedos and long evening dresses, a high-society extravaganza. Present in the audience that evening was a mother with her fidgety nine-year-old son. Weary of waiting, he squirmed constantly in his seat. His mother was in hopes that her son would be encouraged to practice the piano if he could just hear the immortal Paderewski at the keyboard. So—against his wishes—he had come.

As she turned to talk with friends, her son could stay seated no longer. He slipped away from her side, strangely drawn to the ebony concert grand Steinway and its leather tufted stool on the huge stage flooded with blinding lights. Without much notice from the sophisticated audience, the boy sat down at the stool, staring wide-eyed at the black and white keys. He placed his small, trembling fingers in the right location and began to play "chopsticks." The roar of the crowd was hushed as hundreds of frowning faces pointed in his direction. Irritated and embarrassed, they began to shout:

"Get that boy away from there!"

"Who'd bring a kid that young in here?"

"Where's his mother?"

"Somebody stop him!"

Backstage, the master overheard the sounds out front and quickly put together in his mind what was happening. Hurriedly, he grabbed his coat and rushed toward the stage. Without one word of announcement he stooped over behind the boy, reached around both sides, and began to improvise a countermelody to harmonize with and enhance "chopsticks." As the two of them played together, Paderewski kept whispering in the boy's ear:

Keep going. Don't quit. Keep on playing...don't stop...don't quit.

And so it is with us. We hammer away on our project, which seems about as significant as "chopsticks" in a concert hall. And about the time we are ready to give up, along comes the Master, who leans over and whispers:

Now keep going; don't quit. Keep on...don't stop; don't quit, as He improvises on our behalf, providing just the right touch at just the right moment.

The Guest of the Maestro

Max Lucado
with appreciation to Erik Ketcherside
for telling Max the story.

What happens when a dog interrupts a concert? To answer that, come with me to a spring night in Lawrence, Kansas.

Take your seat in Hoch Auditorium and behold the Leipzig Gewandhaus Orchestra—the oldest continually operating orchestra in the world. The greatest composers and conductors in history have directed this orchestra. It was playing in the days of Beethoven (some of the musicians have been replaced).

You watch as stately dressed Europeans take their seats on the stage. You listen as professionals carefully tune their instruments. The percussionist puts her ear to the kettle drum. A violinist plucks the nylon string. A clarinet player tightens the reed. And you sit a bit straighter as the lights dim and the tuning stops. The music is about to begin.

The conductor, dressed in tails, strides onto the stage, springs onto the podium, and gestures for the orchestra to rise. You and two thousand others applaud. The musicians take their seats, the maestro takes his position, and the audience holds its breath.

There is a second of silence between lightning and thunder. And there is a second of silence between the raising of the baton and the explosion of the music. But when it falls the heavens open and you are delightfully drenched in the downpour of Beethoven's Third Symphony.

Such was the power of that spring night in Lawrence, Kansas. That hot, spring night in Lawrence, Kansas. I mention the temperature so you'll understand why the doors were open. It was hot. Hoch Auditorium, a historic building, was not air-conditioned. Combine bright stage lights with formal dress and furious music, and the result is a heated orchestra. Outside doors on each side of the stage were left open in case of a breeze.

Enter, stage right, the dog. A brown, generic, Kansas dog. Not a mean dog. Not a mad dog. Just a curious dog. He passes between the double basses and makes his way through the second violins and into the cellos. His tail wags in beat with the music. As the dog passes between the players, they look at him, look at each other, and continue with the next measure.

The dog takes a liking to a certain cello. Perhaps it was the lateral passing of the bow. Maybe it was the eye-level view of the strings. Whatever it was, it caught the dog's attention and he stopped and watched. The cellist wasn't sure what to do. He'd never played for a canine audience. And music schools don't teach you what dog slobber might do to the lacquer of a sixteenth-century Guarneri cello. But the dog did nothing but watch for a moment and then move on.

Had he passed on through the orchestra, the music might have continued. Had he made his way across the stage into the motioning hands of a stagehand, the audience might never have noticed. But he didn't leave. He stayed. At home in the splendor. Roaming through the meadows of music.

He visited the woodwinds, turned his head at the trumpets, stepped between the flutist's, and stopped by the side of the conductor. And Beethoven's Third Symphony came undone.

The musicians laughed. The audience laughed. The dog looked up at the conductor and panted. And the conductor lowered his baton.

The most historic orchestra in the world. One of the most moving pieces ever written. A night wrapped in glory, all brought to a stop by a wayward dog.

The chuckles ceased as the conductor turned. What fury might erupt? The audience grew quiet as the maestro faced them. What fuse had been lit? The polished, German director looked at the crowd, looked down at the dog, then looked back at the people, raised his hands in a universal gesture and...shrugged.

Everyone roared.

He stepped off the podium and scratched the dog behind the ears. The tail wagged again. The maestro spoke to the dog. He spoke in German, but the dog seemed to understand. The two visited for a few seconds before the maestro took his new friend by the collar and led him off the stage. You'd have thought the dog was Pavarotti the way the people applauded. The conductor returned and the music began and Beethoven seemed none the worse for the whole experience.

Can you find you and me in this picture?

I can. Just call us Fido. And consider God the Maestro.

And envision the moment when we will walk onto his stage. We won't deserve to. We will not have earned it. We may even surprise the musicians with our presence.

The music will be like none we've ever heard. We'll stroll among the angels and listen as they sing. We'll gaze at heaven's lights and gasp as they shine. And we'll walk next to the Maestro, stand by his side, and worship as he leads.

...See the unseen and live for that event. [We are invited] to tune our ears to the song of the skies and long—long for the moment when we'll be at the Maestro's side.

He, too, will welcome. And he, too, will speak. But he will not lead us away. He will invite us to remain, forever his guests on his stage.

Jimmy Durante

Tim Hansel

There's a wonderful story about Jimmy Durante, one of the great entertainers of a generation ago. He was asked to be a part of a show for World War II veterans. He told them his schedule was very busy and he could afford only a few minutes, but if they wouldn't mind his doing one short monologue and immediately leaving for his next appointment, he would come. Of course, the show's director agreed happily.

But when Jimmy got on stage, something interesting happened. He went through the short monologue and then stayed. The applause grew louder and louder and he kept staying. Pretty soon, he had been on fifteen, twenty, then thirty minutes. Finally, he took a last bow and left the stage. Backstage someone stopped him and said, "I thought you had to go after a few minutes. What happened?"

Jimmy answered, "I did have to go, but I can show you the reason I stayed. You can see for yourself if you'll look on the front row." In the front row were two men, each of whom had lost an arm in the war. One had lost his right arm and the other had lost his left. Together, they were able to clap, and that's exactly what they were doing, loudly and cheerfully.

The Day Bart Simpson Prayed

Lee Strobel

Bart wasn't doing well in the fourth grade. When he flunked his book report on *Treasure Island* because he only knew what was on the cover, that was the last straw. His teacher called a meeting with Bart's parents and the school psychiatrist, whose conclusion was that Bart should repeat the fourth grade.

Bart was horrified! "Look at my eyes," he said. "See the sincerity? See the conviction? See the fear? I swear I'll do better!" After all, nothing's worse to a ten-year-old than being held back in school.

But Bart hatched a plan. He made a deal with a brainy student named Martin. He'd teach Martin how to be cool if Martin would help him pass his next American History exam. That final test was monumentally important because if he passed it, Bart would be allowed to graduate.

Bart did teach Martin the fine points of being cool—how to burp on command, how to spray-paint graffiti on garage doors, how to shoot a slingshot at unsuspecting girls. And, sure enough, Martin became the most popular kid in school—so popular, in fact, that he didn't have time to help Bart study.

Now picture this: It was the night before the big test. Bart was sitting at the desk in his room, staring at an open book, trying to study, when he came to the chilling realization that it was too late. He couldn't cram enough into his head in one night to be able to pass the test. Finally, his mom peeked into the room and said, "It's past your bedtime, Bart."

Slowly, Bart closed his book. With the exams just hours away, it seemed like all of his options had evaporated. That's when he got down on his knees next to his bed and prayed to God.

"This is hopeless!" he said. *"Well, [God], I guess this is the end of the road. I know I haven't been a good kid, but if I have to go to school tomorrow, I'll fail the test and be held back. I just need one more day to study, Lord. I need your help! A teacher strike, a power failure, a blizzard—anything that will cancel school tomorrow. I know it's asking a lot, but if anyone can do it, you can. Thanking you in advance, your pal, Bart Simpson."*

The scene switched to an outside view of Bart's house. The lights in his room went out. It was cold and dark. A few moments passed, and then a single snowflake gently fell to the ground. Then another. And another. Suddenly, there was a virtual avalanche of snow; in fact, it was the biggest blizzard in the city's history! The "Hallelujah Chorus" swelled in the background.

The next day, school was cancelled. Bart fought the temptation to go sledding with his friends, and instead studied hard. Then the following day, when the time finally came for the test, he gave it his best shot, but he came up one point short. It looked like he had failed—until at the last possible moment, he miraculously scored one more point and squeaked by with a D minus.

Bart was so happy that he kissed his teacher as he scampered out the door. Homer was so overwhelmed that he posted Bart's paper on the refrigerator and said, "I'm proud of you, boy."

To which Bart replied, "Thanks, Dad. But part of this D minus belongs to God."

Admittedly, Bart's prayer wasn't a perfect model; if you want the best illustration of how to pray, consult Matthew 6:9–13, where Jesus taught His followers how to talk with God. But don't you think Bart did all right for a kid who's more famous for spitballs than spirituality?

See footnote and memo in note section in back of the book.

At the Counter

Tapestry Magazine
Paula Kirk, Editor

This had been a miserable Easter vacation. As I walked through the airport my heart was heavy at the devastation in my daughter's life. Her husband of one year had left her and she was almost immobilized by shock and sorrow. Because she is an air traffic controller, she was now terribly worried about her ability to stay focused.

I stopped to buy souvenirs for my grandchildren back home. While the credit card processed, the smiling clerk asked how I liked her home state.

"It's beautiful," I replied, "but I say that about nearly every place I visit."

"Yes," she nodded, "God has made a beautiful world for us to enjoy. So much variety. What did you see on your vacation?"

Immediately the tears welled up. The grief was raw and close to the surface. "It wasn't a vacation. Just a serious family problem, and my daughter is having an extremely hard time. I hate to leave her," I stammered.

"Oh, but God is good. He will work on your daughter's behalf."

"I know." I whispered back through tears that now flowed freely. From that counter I took away more than my small purchase. I took away a touch of Christ's resurrection power—the power of God's love to reach out and touch a hurting heart.

All the Good Things

Sister Helen P. Mrosla

He was in the first third grade class I taught at Saint Mary's School in Morris, Minn. All 34 of my students were dear to me, but Mark Eklund was one in a million. Very neat in appearance, he had that happy-to-be-alive attitude that made even his occasional mischievousness delightful.

Mark also talked incessantly. I had to remind him again and again that talking without permission was not acceptable. What impressed me so much, though, was his sincere response every time I had to correct him for misbehaving—"Thank you for correcting me, Sister!" I didn't know what to make of it at first, but before long I became accustomed to hearing it many times a day.

One morning my patience was growing thin when Mark talked once too often, and then I made a novice-teacher's mistake. I looked at Mark and said, "If you say one more word, I am going to tape your mouth shut!"

It wasn't ten seconds later when Chuck blurted out, "Mark is talking again." I hadn't asked any of the students to help me watch Mark, but since I had stated the punishment in front of the class, I had to act on it.

I remember the scene as if it had occurred this morning. I walked to my desk, very deliberately opened the drawer and took out a roll of masking tape. Without saying a word, I proceeded to Mark's desk, tore off two pieces of tape and made a big X with them over his mouth. I then returned to the front of the room.

As I glanced at Mark to see how he was doing, he winked at me. That did it! I started laughing. The class cheered as I walked back to Mark's desk, removed the tape, and shrugged my shoulders. His first words were, "Thank you for correcting me, Sister."

At the end of the year I was asked to teach junior-high math. The years flew by, and before I knew it Mark was in my classroom again. He was more handsome than ever and just as polite. Since he had to listen carefully to my instruction in the "new math," he did not talk as much in ninth grade as he had in third.

One Friday, things just didn't feel right. We had worked hard on a new concept all week, and I sensed that the students were growing frustrated with themselves—and edgy with one another. I had to stop this crankiness before it got out of hand. So I asked them to list the names of the other students in the room on two sheets of paper, leaving a space between each name. Then I told them to think of the nicest thing they could say about each of their classmates and write it down.

It took the remainder of the class period to finish the assignment, and as the students left the room, each one handed me the papers. Charlie smiled. Mark said, "Thank you for teaching me, Sister. Have a good weekend."

That Saturday, I wrote down the name of each student on a separate sheet of paper, and I listed what everyone else had said about that individual. On Monday I gave each student his or her list. Before long, the entire class was smiling. "Really?" I heard whispered. "I never knew that meant anything to anyone!" "I didn't know others liked me so much!"

No one ever mentioned those papers in class again. I never knew if they discussed them after class or with their parents, but it didn't matter. The exercise had accomplished its purpose. The students were happy with themselves and one another again.

That group of students moved on. Several years later, after I returned from vacation, my parents met me at the airport.

As we were driving home, Mother asked the usual questions about the trip—the weather, my experiences in general. There was a slight lull in the conversation. Mother gave Dad a sideways glance and simply said, "Dad?" My father cleared his throat as he usually did before something important. "The Eklunds called last night," he began.

"Really?" I said. "I haven't heard from them in years. I wonder how Mark is."

Dad responded quietly. "Mark was killed in Vietnam," he said. "The funeral is tomorrow, and his parents would like it if you could attend." To this day I can still point to the exact spot on I-494 where Dad told me about Mark.

I had never seen a serviceman in a military coffin before. Mark looked so handsome, so mature. All I could think at that moment was, *Mark, I would give all the masking tape in the world if only you would talk to me.*

The church was packed with Mark's friends. Chuck's sister sang "The Battle Hymn of the Republic." Why did it have to rain on the day of the funeral? It was difficult enough at the graveside. The pastor said the usual prayers, and the bugler played taps. One by one those who loved Mark took a last walk by the coffin....

I was the last one.... As I stood there, one of the soldiers who had acted as pallbearer came up to me. "Were you Mark's math teacher?" he asked. I nodded as I continued to stare at the coffin. "Mark talked about you a lot," he said.

After the funeral, most of Mark's former classmates headed to Chuck's farmhouse for lunch. Mark's mother and father were there, obviously waiting for me. "We want to show you something," his father said, taking a wallet out of his pocket. "They found this on Mark when he was killed. We thought you might recognize it."

Opening the billfold, he carefully removed two worn pieces of notebook paper that had obviously been taped, folded and refolded many times. I knew without looking that the papers were the ones on which I had listed all the good things each of Mark's classmates had said about him. "Thank you so much for doing that," Mark's mother said. "As you can see, Mark treasured it."

Mark's classmates started to gather around us. Charlie smiled rather sheepishly and said, "I still have my list. It's in the top drawer of my desk at home." Chuck's wife said, "Chuck asked me to put his in our wedding album." "I have mine too," Marilyn said. "It's in my diary." Then Vicki, another classmate, reached into her pocketbook, took out her wallet and showed her worn and frazzled list to the group. "I carry this with me at all times," Vicki said without batting an eyelash. "I think we all saved our lists."

That's when I finally sat down and cried. I cried for Mark and for all his friends who would never see him again.

The Hand

Author unknown

A Thanksgiving Day editorial in the newspaper told of a school teacher who asked her first-graders to draw a picture of something they were thankful for. She thought of how little these children from poor neighborhoods actually had to be thankful for. But she knew that most of them would draw pictures of turkeys on tables with food. The teacher was taken aback with the picture Douglas handed in...a simple childishly drawn hand.

But whose hand? This class was captivated by the abstract image. "I think it must be the hand of God that brings us food," said one child. "A farmer," said another, "because he grows the turkeys." Finally when the others were back at work the teacher bent over Douglas's desk and asked whose hand it was. "It's your hand, Teacher," he mumbled.

She recalled that frequently at recess she had taken Douglas, a scrubby forlorn child, by the hand. She often did that with the children. But it meant so much to Douglas. Perhaps this was everyone's Thanksgiving, not for the material things given to us but for the chance, in whatever small way, to give to others.

The Kiss

Richard Selzer

I stand by the bed where a young woman lies, her face post-operative, her mouth twisted in palsy; clownish. A tiny twig of the facial nerve, the one to the muscles of her mouth, has been severed. She will be thus from now on. The surgeon had followed with religious fervor the curve of her flesh; I promise you that. Nevertheless, to remove the tumor from her cheek, I had cut the little nerve. Her young husband is in the room. He stands on the opposite side of the bed, and together they seem to dwell in the evening lamplight, isolated from me, private. *Who are they*, I ask myself, *he and this wry-mouth I have made, who gaze at and touch each other so generously, greedily?*

"Will my mouth always be like this?" she asks.

"Yes," I say, "it will be. It is because the nerve was cut."

She nods and is silent. But the young man smiles. "I like it," he says. "It is kind of cute."

All at once I know who he is. I understand, and I lower my gaze. One is not bold in an encounter with [such love]. Unmindful, he bends to kiss her crooked mouth, and I am so close I can see how he twists his own lips to accommodate her, to show her that their kiss still works.

Changed Lives

Tim Kimmel

In 1921 Lewis Lawes became the warden at Sing Sing Prison. No prison was tougher than Sing Sing during that time. But when Warden Lawes retired some 20 years later, that prison had become a humanitarian institution. Those who studied the system said credit for the change belonged to Lawes. But when he was asked about the transformation, here's what he said: "I owe it all to my wonderful wife, Catherine, who is buried outside the prison walls."

Catherine Lawes was a young mother with three small children when her husband became the warden. Everybody warned her from the beginning that she should never set foot inside the prison walls, but that didn't stop Catherine! When the first prison basketball game was held, she went...walking into the gym with her three beautiful kids and she sat in the stands with the inmates.

Her attitude was: "My husband and I are going to take care of these men and I believe they will take care of me! I don't have to worry!"

She insisted on getting acquainted with them and their records. She discovered one convicted murderer was blind so she paid him a visit. Holding his hand in hers she said, "Do you read Braille?"

"What's Braille?" he asked. Then she taught him how to read. Years later he would weep in love for her.

Later, Catherine found a deaf-mute in prison. She went to school to learn how to use sign language. Many said that Catherine Lawes was the body of Jesus that came alive again in Sing Sing from 1921 to 1937.

Then, she was killed in a car accident. The next morning Lewis Lawes didn't come to work, so the acting warden took his place. It seemed almost instantly that the prison knew something was wrong.

The following day, her body was resting in a casket in her home, three-quarters of a mile from the prison. As the acting warden took his early morning walk he was shocked to see a large crowd of the toughest, hardest-looking criminals gathered like a herd of animals at the main gate. He came closer and noted tears of grief and sadness. He knew how much they loved Catherine. He turned and faced the men, "All right, men, you can go. Just be sure and check in tonight!" Then he opened the gate and a parade of criminals walked, without a guard, the three-quarters of a mile to stand in line to pay their final respects to Catherine Lawes. And every one of them checked back in. Every one!

HUGS

A hug is the perfect gift
One size fits all
And no one minds if you exchange it.

The Passerby

Hester Tetreault

I saw him most mornings when I looked out of the living room window. He became part of my day. Slightly bent, he dragged one leg a little, the foot twisted so that he walked more on the side of his foot than the sole. I guessed he was in his eighties. He wore only a flannel shirt. When I could see his breath against the air on a frosty morning, I wondered if he was cold.

While working in the garden one morning, I saw the old man smile and tousle the hair of a small boy who passed by him on his way into school.

"It's now or never," I decided, emboldened to cross the street and introduce myself.

His pale blue eyes enlivened and his face wrinkled in another smile. This time for me. "My wife and I are from Switzerland. We came first to Canada and then to America, many years ago," he told me. "We work very hard. In time we save enough to buy our own farm. I do not speak English so good, so I pick up children's first readers and secretly I study until I learn," he laughed. He gazed toward the elementary school beyond the wire fence, and his face grew solemn. "We never had any children."

I pondered the conversation in the quiet of the day, touched deeply by the loneliness in his voice as he spoke of the few remaining relatives in his native homeland, distanced not only by miles, but by lives lived worlds apart.

"My wife is not so good," he told me when I asked about her.

I wanted to jump in, offer help, be a friend, but I had already pushed myself upon this stranger. Reserve ruled the moment. I pointed to my house. "Please," I said, leaving the next overture to his discretion, "stop in and have a cup of coffee with me sometime when you are out walking."

I didn't see him after that, but I thought about him often. Was he housebound or sick? Had his wife's health deteriorated suddenly? If only I knew his name, or where he lived. My invitation mocked me with its ineptitude. I had so wanted to be a friend.

Months went by before I saw him again. On an errand, and only fifteen minutes' walk from home, I saw the familiar limp and swing. He moved slowly, shoulders slumped, and one foot twisted so that the heel did not stay in his shoe. His pale face was thinner than I remembered, but his eyes still twinkled, and he smiled in recognition as I reintroduced myself. I learned his name was Paul.

"I don't walk as far as I used to," he explained, "my wife, I cannot leave her very long. Her mind is going," he grimaced with a touch to his forehead, "she forgets things." He gestured toward a green and white wood-framed house across the street and said, "would you like to come in and see my drawings?"

"I'm on my way to pick up my car from the garage," I said regretfully, "but I'd love to see them another time."

"You come this evening, then?" He looked hopeful.

"Oh, yes," I said, "I'll come this evening."

The pungent smell of damp fir needles permeated the chill, sulky evening air. Paul stood expectantly by the window. When he opened the door, he was groomed for company.

His wife, slender and frail, came from the kitchen, tucking wisps of white hair back into a tidy bun. "Come in, come in," she bid, with a smile full of the grace of her generation. She reached out a worn, soft hand.

"This," Paul said, "is my wife, Bertha." He straightened and grew in stature. "We've been married fifty-six years."

That evening I was introduced to Paul's pen and ink sketches. We went from room to room. Pictures hung in modest frames, pages were tucked in drawers. There were sketches of celebrities, scenes, anything that took his fancy. Each had a story.

But the compelling story was the harsh reality of talent ignored for people like him of that generation. "It won't put bread on the table," his father told him. "If you sit around drawing like that you'll never amount to anything."

His mother died when he was nine. He remembered the gentle tap of her stick against his head whenever she found him with pad and pencil in hand. "Make yourself useful. Don't waste your time." she chided.

When we returned to the kitchen, Bertha searched for some tangible expression of her hospitality. "I wish I had cookies to offer you. I can't cook like I used to."

"I couldn't eat a thing, I just finished dinner," I said.

Their dinner was "meals on wheels," three days a week. "We cannot eat so much. We have plenty for the next day. Except Mondays. Mondays we try to cook for ourselves."

They wanted me to stay awhile. We sat and talked. Dignity filled their house.

Paul answered the door the following Monday. His eyes fell on the tray I carried.

He was glad I'd come, but his pinched and agitated face told me I'd stumbled upon an outburst of anger.

Bertha, pale and flustered, gathered herself. "We're not feeling so good today, and I'm having trouble with my head and remembering." She threw her hands up. "I don't know what it is...old age!"

They led me into the kitchen. Canned soup dripped where it spilled over the stove.

Paul's hands shook as he showed me the hole scorched in his shirt sleeve as he tried to cope with a meal. The flare-up, cut short by my arrival, had taken its toll. He put his hand to his forehead and sighed, gaining equilibrium. "It's just that she upsets me sometimes," he said, arranging the knives and forks on the table as I set out the lunch I had cooked.

Bertha still fretted to know where she had put the wooden spoon he no longer needed, and my heart ached for her.

Frailty of age, its irritability, frustrations, limitations and fears had been too much for them both that morning. Impassioned by their need, I reached for Bertha's trembling hand. "Could we sit down and pray?" I asked.

"Oh," Bertha exclaimed, "that's what we need more of."

Paul joined us in a chair beside the couch.

After I prayed for them I looked up. Gratitude and relief flooded their faces. All tension was gone. I hugged them both and delighted in the hugs I received in return.

"You are too good to us," Paul said, making his way to the dining room table and pulling out a chair for his wife.

No, I thought, *God is too good to me. He allowed me to share this moment as He touched two people He loves very much.* How blessed I was in the process. I wanted to be their friend, and He had given me the desire of my heart.

Just a Kid with Cerebral Palsy

Tony Campolo

I was asked to be a counselor in a junior high camp. Everybody ought to be a counselor in a junior high camp—just once. A junior high kid's concept of a good time is picking on people. And in this particular case, at this particular camp, there was a little boy who was suffering from cerebral palsy. His name was Billy. And they picked on him.

Oh, they picked on him. As he walked across the camp with his uncoordinated body they would line up and imitate his grotesque movements. I watched him one day as he was asking for direction. "Which...way is...the...craft...shop?" he stammered, his mouth contorting. And the boys mimicked in that same awful stammer, "It's...over...there...Billy." And then they laughed at him. I was irate.

But my furor reached its highest pitch when on Thursday morning it was Billy's cabin's turn to give devotions. I wondered what would happen, because they had appointed Billy to be the speaker. I knew that they just wanted to get him up there to make fun of him. As he dragged his way to the front, you could hear the giggles rolling over the crowd. It took little Billy almost five minutes to say seven words.

"Jesus...loves...me...and...I...love...Jesus."

When he finished, there was dead silence. I looked over my shoulder and saw junior high boys bawling all over the place. A revival broke out in that camp after Billy's short testimony. And as I travel all over the world, I find missionaries and preachers who say, "Remember me? I was converted at that junior high camp." We counselors had tried everything to get those kids interested in Jesus. We even imported baseball players whose batting averages had gone up since they had started praying. But God chose not to use the superstars. He chose a kid with cerebral palsy to break the spirits of the haughty. He's that kind of God.

REPEAT PERFORMANCE
Nancy Spiegelberg

O God of Second Chances
and New Beginnings,

Here I am again.

Virtues

ACT MEDIUM

Leslie B. Flynn

The children worked long and hard on their own little cardboard shack. It was to be a special spot—a clubhouse—where they could meet in solemn assembly or just laugh, play games, and fool around. As they thought long and hard about their rules, they came up with three rather perceptive ones:

1. *Nobody act big.*
2. *Nobody act small.*
3. *Everybody act medium.*

Valentines

Dale Galloway

L ittle Chad was a shy, quiet young fella. One day he came home and told his mother he'd like to make a valentine for everyone in his class. Her heart sank. She thought, *I wish he wouldn't do that!* because she had watched the children when they walked home from school. Her Chad was always behind them. They laughed and hung on to each other and talked to each other. But Chad was never included. Nevertheless, she decided she would go along with her son. So she purchased the paper and glue and crayons. For three whole weeks, night after night, Chad painstakingly made thirty-five valentines.

Valentine's Day dawned, and Chad was beside himself with excitement! He carefully stacked them up, put them in a bag, and bolted out the door. His mom decided to bake him his favorite cookies and serve them up warm and nice with a cool glass of milk when he came home from school. She just knew he would be disappointed...maybe that would ease the pain a little. It hurt her to think that he wouldn't get many valentines—maybe none at all.

That afternoon she had the cookies and milk on the table. When she heard the children outside she looked out the window. Sure enough here they came, laughing and having the best time. And, as always, there was Chad in the rear. He walked a little faster than usual. She fully expected him to burst into tears as soon as he got inside. His arms were empty, she noticed, and when the door opened she choked back the tears.

"Mommy has some warm cookies and milk for you."

But he hardly heard her words. He just marched right on by, his face aglow, and all he could say was:

"Not a one...not a one."

And then he added, "I didn't forget a one, not a single one!'"

CHOOSING

Victor E. Frankl

Dr. Victor E. Frankl, survivor of three grim years at Auschwitz and other Nazi prisons, has recorded his observations on life in Hitler's camps:

We who lived in concentration camps can remember the men who walked through the huts comforting others, giving away their last piece of bread. They have been few in number, but they offer sufficient proof that everything can be taken from a man but one thing: the last of the human freedoms—to choose one's attitude in any given set of circumstances, to choose one's own way.

It's a Start
Gary Smalley and John Trent

We know a wealthy couple in Dallas who have really struggled with teaching their children servanthood. For one thing, the kids have had almost whatever they've wanted for years. They've become so accustomed to others meeting their needs that the idea of "serving" sounded like something from the Middle Ages...or Mars.

The father in that family realized he was getting a late start, but hey, it was better than no start at all!

A week or so before the holidays, he said to his family, "We're going to do something different this Thanksgiving."

His teenagers sat up and listened. Usually when he said things like that it meant something exotic. Like para-sailing in the Bahamas.

But not this time. "We're going to go down to the mission," he told them, "and we're going to serve Thanksgiving dinner to some poor and homeless people."

"We're going to what?"

"Come on, Dad, you're kidding...aren't you? Tell us you're kidding."

He wasn't. They went along with it because of his firm insistence, but no one was happy about it. For some reason their Dad had "gotten weird" and apparently it was something he just had to get out of his system. Serving at the mission! What if their friends heard about it?

No one could have predicted what happened that day. And no one in the family could remember when they had a better time together. They hustled around the kitchen, dished up turkey and dressing, sliced pumpkin pie and refilled countless coffee cups. They clowned around with the little kids and listened to old folks tell stories of Thanksgivings long ago and far away.

The dad in the family was thoroughly pleased (would you believe stunned?) by the way his kids responded. But nothing could have prepared him for their request a few weeks later.

"Dad...we want to go back to the mission and serve Christmas dinner!"

And they did. As the kids hoped, they met some of the same people they'd become acquainted with at Thanksgiving. One needy family in particular had been on their minds, and they all lit up when they saw them back in the chow line again. Since that time, the families have had several contacts. The pampered teenagers have rolled up their sleeves more than once to serve the family from one of Dallas's poorer neighborhoods.

There was a marked but subtle change in that home. The kids didn't seem to be taking things for granted anymore. Their parents found them more serious...more responsible. Yes, it was a late start. But it was a start.

What's It Like in Your Town?

Retold by Kris Gray

Once there was an old and very wise man. Every day he would sit outside a gas station in his rocking chair and wait to greet motorists as they passed through his small town. On this day, his granddaughter knelt down at the foot of his chair and slowly passed the time with him.

As they sat and watched the people come and go, a tall man who surely had to be a tourist—since they knew everyone in the town—began looking around as if he were checking out the area for a place to live. The stranger walked up and asked, "So what kind of town is this that we're in?" The older gentleman slowly turned to the man and replied, "Well, what kind of town are you from?" The tourist said, "In the town I'm from everyone is very critical of each other. The neighbors all gossip about everyone, and it's a real negative place to live. I'm sure glad to be leaving. It is not a very cheerful place." The man in the chair looked at the stranger and said, "You know, that's just how this town is."

An hour or so later a family that was also passing through stopped for gas. The car slowly turned in and rolled to a stop in front of where the older gentleman and his granddaughter were sitting. The mother jumped out with two small children and asked where the restrooms were. The man in the chair pointed to a small, bent-up sign that was barely hanging by one nail on the side of the door. The father stepped out of the car and also asked the man, "Is this town a pretty good place to live?" The man in the chair replied, "What about the town you are from? How is it?" The father looked at him and said, "Well, in the town I'm from everyone is very close and always willing to lend their neighbor a helping hand. There's always a hello and thank-you everywhere you go. I really hate to leave. I feel almost like we are leaving family." The older gentlemen turned to the father and gave him a warm smile. "You know, that's a lot like this small town." Then the family returned to the car, said their thank-yous, waved goodbye and drove away.

After the family was in the distance, the granddaughter looked up at her grandfather and asked, "Grandpa, how come when the first man came into our town you told him it was a terrible place to live and when the family came in to town you told them it was a wonderful place to live?" The grandfather lovingly looked down at his granddaughter's wondering blue eyes and said, "No matter where you move, you take your own attitude with you and that's what makes it terrible or wonderful."

The Experiment

Catherine Marshall
Retold by Marilyn K. McAuley

Catherine Marshall tells of the time she decided to do a one-day experiment. Oh, it really was an eye-opener for her. You see, she had a problem common to most of us. She found it too easy to be critical of others. Well, one morning as she meditated on the verse, "So don't criticize each other anymore," (Romans 14:13, TLB) she became aware of the Lord nudging her to not be critical for one day.

Of course she tried to shove it off. But she couldn't get it out of her mind. So she tried to rationalize her critical attitude. After all, aren't we to use the intelligence God gave us to analyze and evaluate—even though the result is not always positive? The nudging continued right through the debate going on in her mind until she finally agreed to give the experiment a try—but just for the one day would she fast from criticism.

Through most of the morning she kept wondering what the result would be at the end of the day. The lunch with her husband and friends was normal except for the unusual silence of one person—Catherine. She had not committed to silence, just to not criticizing. It surprised her to realize how much of her conversation was usually critical and judgmental. She was silent only because she couldn't contribute to the conversation without judging. So, she kept quiet and no one seemed to notice. A sting to the pride as well.

It wasn't until mid-afternoon that something special began to happen. The floodgate of ideas began to open and creative thoughts flowed through in a way she hadn't experienced in a long time.

At day's end she marveled at all that had transpired simply because she refused to entertain a critical attitude. A letter to encourage a friend, insight into praying for a college student, seeking her child's forgiveness, all filtered through her freely because there were no negative thoughts to stop them.

Catherine's one-day experiment became a lifetime habit.

It Really Didn't Matter

Charles Colson

The young people at Shively Christian Church, led at the time by Youth Pastor Dave Stone, were fiercely competitive with their neighbor, Shively Baptist, in all things, especially softball. They were also serious about their Christianity, faithfully attending the summer Bible camp led by the youth pastor.

One week the Bible lesson was about Jesus washing His disciples' feet, from John 13. To make the servanthood lesson stick, Pastor Stone divided the kids into groups and told them to go out and find a practical way to be servants.

"I want you to be Jesus in the city for the next two hours," he said. "If Jesus were here, what would He do? Figure out how He would help people."

Two hours later the kids reconvened in Pastor Stone's living room to report what they had done.

One group had done two hours of yard work for an elderly man. Another group bought ice cream treats and delivered them to several widows in the church. A third group visited a church member in the hospital and gave him a card. Another group went to a nursing home and sang Christmas carols— yes, Christmas carols in the middle of August. One elderly resident remarked that it was the warmest Christmas she could remember.

But when the fifth group stood up and reported what they had done, everyone groaned. This group had made its way to none other than their arch rival, Shively Baptist, where they had asked the pastor if he knew someone who needed help. The pastor sent them to the home of an elderly woman who needed yard work done. There, for two hours, they mowed grass, raked the yard, and trimmed hedges.

When they were getting ready to leave, the woman called

the group together and thanked them for their hard work. "I don't know how I could get along without you," she told them. "You kids at Shively Baptist are always coming to my rescue."

"Shively *Baptist!*" interrupted Pastor Stone. "I sure hope you set her straight and told her you were from Shively *Christian* Church."

"Why, no, we didn't," the kids said. "We didn't think it mattered."

Monuments

Charles Allen

In Hiawatha, Kansas, in the Mt. Hope Cemetery stands a strange group of gravestones. A guy named Davis, a farmer and self-made man, had them erected. He began as a lowly hired hand and by sheer determination and frugality he managed to amass a considerable fortune in his lifetime. In the process, however, the farmer did not make many friends. Nor was he close to his wife's family, since they thought she had married beneath her dignity. Embittered, he vowed never to leave his in-laws a thin dime.

When his wife died, Davis erected an elaborate statue in her memory. He hired a sculptor to design a monument which showed both her and him at opposite ends of a love seat. He was so pleased with the result that he commissioned another statue—this time of himself, kneeling at her grave, placing a wreath on it. That impressed him so greatly that he planned a third monument, this time of his wife kneeling at his future gravesite, depositing a wreath. He had the sculptor add a pair of wings on her back, since she was no longer alive, giving her the appearance of an angel. One idea led to another until he'd spent no less than a quarter million dollars on the monuments to himself and his wife!

Whenever someone from the town would suggest he might be interested in a community project (a hospital, a park and swimming pool for the children, a municipal building, etc.), the old miser would frown, set his jaw, and shout back, "What's this town ever done for me? I don't owe this town nothin'!"

After using up all his resources on stone statues and selfish pursuits, John Davis died at 92, a grim-faced resident of the poorhouse. But his monuments...it's strange....Each one is slowly sinking into the Kansas soil, fast becoming victims of time, vandalism, and neglect. Monuments of spite. Sad reminders of a self-centered, unsympathetic life. There is a certain poetic justice in the fact that within a few years, they will all be gone.

Oh, by the way, very few people attended Mr. Davis' funeral. It is reported that only one person seemed genuinely moved by any sense of personal loss. He was Horace England...the tombstone salesman.

Chickens

Anne Paden

Jack London's wonderful classic, *White Fang*, tells the story of an animal, half dog-half wolf, as he survives his life in the wild and then learns to live among men. There is one story in particular that has left a lasting impression on my heart.

White Fang was very fond of chickens and on one occasion raided a chicken-roost and killed fifty hens. His master, Weeden Scott, whom White Fang saw as man-God and "loved with single heart," scolded him and then took him into the chicken yard. When White Fang saw his favorite food walking around right in front of him he obeyed his natural impulse and lunged for a chicken. He was immediately checked by his master's voice. They stayed in the chicken yard for quite a while and every time White Fang made a move toward a chicken his master's voice would stop him. In this way he learned what his master wanted—he had learned to ignore the chickens.

Weeden Scott's father argued that you "couldn't cure a chicken killer," but Weeden challenged him and they agreed to lock White Fang in with the chickens all afternoon.

Locked in the yard and there deserted by the master, White Fang lay down and went to sleep. Once he got up and walked over to the trough for a drink of water. The chickens he calmly ignored. So far as he was concerned they did not exist. At four o'clock he executed a running jump, gained the roof of the chicken house and leaped to the ground outside, whence he sauntered gravely to the house. He had learned the law.

Out of love and a desire to obey his master's will, White Fang overcame his natural, inborn desires. He may not have understood the reason but he chose to bend his will to his master's.

Animal stories have a way of breaking your heart and often reveal a profound truth. The simplicity and purity of White Fang's love and devotion to his master help me realize that my life will always be full of "chickens." What I have to settle is, whom will I serve?

The Millionaire and the Scrublady

William E. Barton
(*Unusual typesetting from original text.*)

There is a certain Millionaire, who hath his Offices on the Second Floor of the First National Bank Building. And when he goeth up to his Offices he rideth in the Elevator, but when he goeth down, then he walketh.

And he is an Haughty Man, who once was poor, and hath risen in the World. He is a Self-made Man who worshipeth his maker.

And he payeth his Rent regularly on the first day of the month, and he considereth not that there are Human Beings who run the Elevators, and who Clean the Windows, hanging at a great height above the Sidewalk, and who shovel Coal into the furnaces under the Boilers. Neither doth he at Christmas time remember any of them with a Tip or a Turkey.

And there is in that Building a Poor Woman who Scrubbeth the Stairs and the Halls. And he hath walked past her often but hath never seen her until Recently. For his head was high in the air, and he was thinking of More Millions.

Now it came to pass on a day that he left his Office, and started to walk down the Stairs.

And the Scrublady was halfway down; for she had begun at the top and was giving the stairs their First Onceover. And upon the topmost Stair, in a wet and soapy spot, there was a Large Cake of Soap. And the Millionaire stepped on it.

Now the foot which he set upon the Soap flew eastward toward the sunrise, and the other foot started on an expedition of its own toward the going down of the Sun. And the Millionaire sat down on the Topmost Step, but he did not remain there. As it had been his intention to Descend, so he

Descended, but not in the manner of his Original Design. And as he descended he struck each step with a sound as if it had been a Drum.

And the Scrublady stood aside courteously, and let him go.

And at the bottom he arose, and considered whether he should rush into the Office of the Building and demand that the Scrublady should be fired; but he considered that if he should tell the reason there would be great Mirth among the occupants of the Building. And so he held his peace.

But since that day he taketh notice of the Scrublady, and passeth her with Circumspection.

For there is no one so high or mighty that he can afford to ignore any of his fellow human beings. For a very Humble Scrublady and a very common bar of Yellow Soap can take the mind of a Great Man off his Business Troubles with surprising rapidity.

Wherefore, consider these things, and count not thyself too high above even the humblest of the children of God.

Lest haply thou come down from thy place of pride and walk off with thy bruises aching a little more by reason of thy suspicion that the Scrublady is Smiling in her Suds, and facing the day's work the more cheerfully by reason of the fun thou hast afforded her.

For these are solemn days, and he that bringeth a smile to the face of a Scrublady hath not lived in vain.

The Signal

Retold by Alice Gray

The young man sat alone on the bus and most of the time stared out the window. He was in his mid-twenties, nice looking with a kind face. His dark blue shirt matched the color of his eyes. His hair was short and neat. Occasionally he would look away from the window and the anxiety on his young face touched the heart of the grandmotherly woman sitting across the aisle. The bus was just approaching the outskirts of a small town when she was so drawn to the young man that she scooted across the aisle and asked permission to sit next to him.

After a few moments of small talk about the warm spring weather, he blurted out, "I've been in prison for two years. I just got out this morning and I'm going home." His words tumbled out as he told her he was raised in a poor but proud family and how his crime had brought his family shame and heartbreak. In the whole two years he had not heard from them. He knew they were too poor to travel the distance to where he had been in prison and his parents probably felt too uneducated to write. He had stopped writing them when no answers came.

Three weeks before being released, he desperately wrote one more letter to his family. He told them how sorry he was for disappointing them and asked for their forgiveness.

He went on to explain about being released from prison and that he would take the bus to his hometown—the one that goes right by the front yard of the house where he grew up and where his parents still lived. In his letter, he said he would understand if they wouldn't forgive him.

He wanted to make it easy for them and so asked them to give him a signal that he could see from the bus. If they had forgiven him and wanted him to come back home, they could tie a white ribbon on the old apple tree that stood in the front yard. If the signal wasn't there, he would stay on the bus, leave town and be out of their lives forever.

As the bus neared his street, the young man became more and more anxious to the point he was afraid to look out the window because he was so sure there would be no ribbon.

After listening to his story, the woman asked simply, "Would it help if we traded seats and I'll sit near to the window and look for you?" The bus traveled a few more blocks and then she saw the tree. She gently touched the young man's shoulder and choking back tears said, "Look! Oh look! The whole tree is covered with white ribbons."

RESEMBLANCE

Author unknown

We are most like beasts when we kill.
We are most like men when we judge.
We are most like God when we forgive.

A Gift from the Heart

Norman Vincent Peale
Reprinted with permission from
January 1968 Readers Digest

New York City, where I live, is impressive at any time, but as Christmas approaches, it's overwhelming. Store windows blaze with light and color, furs and jewels. Golden angels, 40 feet tall, hover over Fifth Avenue. Wealth, power, opulence—nothing in the world can match this fabulous display.

Through the gleaming canyons, people hurry to find last-minute gifts. Money seems to be no problem. If there's a problem, it's that the recipients so often have everything they need or want that it's hard to find anything suitable, anything that will really say, "I love you."

Last December, as Christ's birthday drew near, a stranger was faced with just that problem. She had come from Switzerland to live in an American home and perfect her English. In return, she was willing to act as secretary, mind the grandchildren, do anything that was asked. She was just a girl in her late teens. Her name was Ursula.

One of the tasks her employers gave Ursula was keeping track of Christmas presents as they arrived. There were many, and all would require acknowledgment. Ursula kept a faithful record, but with a growing concern. She was grateful to her American friends; she wanted to show her gratitude by giving them a Christmas present. But nothing that she could buy with her small allowance could compare with the gifts she was recording daily. Besides, even without these gifts, it seemed that her employers already had everything.

At night, from her window, Ursula could see the snowy expanse of Central Park, and beyond it the jagged skyline of the city. Far below, in the restless streets, taxis hooted and traffic lights winked red and green. It was so different from the silent majesty of the Alps that at times she had to blink back tears of the homesickness she was careful never to show. It was in the solitude of her little room, a few days before Christmas, that a secret idea came to Ursula.

It was almost as if a voice spoke clearly, inside her head. "It's true," said the voice, "that many people in this city have much more than you do. But surely there are many who have far less. If you will think about this, you may find a solution to what's troubling you."

Ursula thought long and hard. Finally on her day off, which was Christmas Eve, she went to a great department store. She moved slowly along the crowded aisles, selecting and rejecting things in her mind. At last she bought something, and had it wrapped in gaily colored paper. She went out into the gray twilight and looked helplessly around. Finally, she went up to a doorman, resplendent in blue and gold. "Excuse me, please," she said in her hesitant English, "can you tell me where to find a poor street?"

"A poor street, miss?" said the puzzled man.

"Yes, a very poor street. The poorest in the city."

The doorman looked doubtful. "Well, you might try Harlem. Or down in the Village. Or the Lower East Side, maybe."

But these names meant nothing to Ursula. She thanked the doorman and walked along, threading her way through the stream of shoppers until she came to a tall policeman. "Please," she said, "can you direct me to a very poor street...in Harlem?"

The policeman looked at her sharply and shook his head. "Harlem's no place for you, miss." And he blew his whistle and sent the traffic swirling past.

Holding her package carefully, Ursula walked on, head bowed against the sharp wind. If a street looked poorer than the one she was on, she took it. But none seemed like the slums she had heard about. Once she stopped a woman, "Please, where do the very poor people live?" But the woman gave her a hard stare and hurried on.

Darkness came sifting from the sky. Ursula was cold and discouraged and afraid of becoming lost. She came to an intersection and stood forlornly on the corner. What she was trying to do suddenly seemed foolish, impulsive, absurd. Then, through the traffic's roar, she heard the cheerful tinkle of a bell. On the corner opposite, a Salvation Army man was making his holiday traditional Christmas appeal.

At once Ursula felt better; The Salvation Army was a part of life in Switzerland, too. Surely this man could tell her what she wanted to know. She waited for the light, then crossed over to him. "Can you help me? I'm looking for a baby. I have here a little present for the poorest baby I can find." And she held up the package with the green ribbon and the gaily colored paper.

Dressed in gloves and overcoat a size too big for him, he seemed a very ordinary man. But behind his steel-rimmed glasses his eyes were kind. He looked at Ursula and stopped ringing his bell. "What sort of present?" he asked.

"A little dress. For a small, poor baby. Do you know of one?"

"Oh, yes," he said. "Of more than one, I'm afraid."

"Is it far away? I could take a taxi maybe?"

The Salvation Army man wrinkled his forehead. Finally he said, "It's almost six o'clock. My relief will show up then. If you want to wait, and you can afford a dollar taxi ride, I'll take you to a family in my own neighborhood who needs just about everything."

"And they have a small baby?"

"A very small baby."

"Then," said Ursula joyfully, "I wait!"

The substitute bell-ringer came. A cruising taxi slowed. In its welcome warmth, she told her new friend about herself, how she came to be in New York, what she was trying to do. He listened in silence, and the taxi driver listened too. When they reached their destination, the driver said, "Take your time, miss. I'll wait for you."

On the sidewalk, Ursula stared up at the forbidding tenement—dark, decaying, saturated with hopelessness. A gust of wind, iron-cold, stirred the refuse in the street and rattled the reeling ashcans. "They live on the third floor," the Salvation Army man said. "Shall we go up?"

But Ursula shook her head. "They would try to thank me, and this is not from me." She pressed the package into his hand. "Take it up for me, please. Say it's from...from someone who has everything."

The taxi bore her swiftly from the dark streets to lighted ones, from misery to abundance. She tried to visualize the Salvation Army man climbing the stairs, the knock, the explanation, the package being opened, the dress on the baby. It was hard to do.

Arriving at the apartment on Fifth Avenue where she lived, she fumbled in her purse. But the driver flicked the flag up. "No charge, miss."

"No charge?" echoed Ursula, bewildered.

"Don't worry," the driver said. "I've been paid." He smiled at her and drove away.

Ursula was up early the next day. She set the table with special care. By the time she was finished, the family was awake, and there was all the excitement and laughter of Christmas morning. Soon the living room was a sea of gay discarded wrappings. Ursula thanked everyone for the presents she received. Finally, when there was a lull, she began to explain hesitantly why there seemed to be none from her. She told about going to the department store. She told about the

Salvation Army man. She told about the taxi driver. When she was finished, there was a long silence. No one seemed to trust himself to speak. "So you see," said Ursula, "I try to do kindness in your name. And this is my Christmas present to you."

How do I know all this? I know it because ours was the home where Ursula lived. Ours was the Christmas she shared. We were like many Americans, so richly blessed that to this child there seemed to be nothing she could add to all the material things we already had. And so she offered something of far greater value: a gift from the heart, an act of kindness carried out in our name.

Strange, isn't it? A shy Swiss girl, alone in a great impersonal city. You would think that nothing she could do would affect anyone. And yet, by trying to give away love, she brought the true spirit of Christmas into our lives, the spirit of selfless giving. That was Ursula's secret—and she shared it with us all.

Thankful in Everything?

Matthew Henry

Matthew Henry is a well-known Bible commentator. One day he was robbed and that evening made the following entry in his diary:

Let me be thankful—
first, because I was never robbed before
second, because although they took my wallet they did not take
   my life
third, because although they took my all, it was not much
and fourth, because it was I who was robbed, not I who robbed.

The Good Samaritan

Tim Hansel

One semester, a seminary professor set up his preaching class in an unusual way. He scheduled his students to preach on the Parable of the Good Samaritan and on the day of the class, he choreographed his experiment so that each student would go, one at a time, from one classroom to another where he or she would preach a sermon. The professor gave some students ten minutes to go from one room to the other; to others he allowed less time, forcing them to rush in order to meet the schedule. Each student, one at a time, had to walk down a certain corridor and pass by a bum, who was deliberately planted there, obviously in need of some sort of aid.

The results were surprising, and offered a powerful lesson to them. The percentage of those good men and women who stopped to help was extremely low, especially for those who were under the pressure of a shorter time period. The tighter the schedule, the fewer were those who stopped to help the indigent man. When the professor revealed his experiment, you can imagine the impact on that class of future spiritual leaders. Rushing to preach a sermon on the Good Samaritan they had walked past the beggar at the heart of the parable. We must have eyes to see as well as hands to help, or we may never help at all. I think this well-known poem expresses it powerfully:

> I was hungry and you formed a humanities club
> to discuss my hunger.
> Thank you.
> I was imprisoned and you crept off quietly
> to your chapel to pray for my release.
> Nice.

I was naked and in your mind you debated the
morality of my appearance.
What good did that do?
I was sick and you knelt and thanked God for
your health.
But I needed you.
I was homeless and you preached to me of the
shelter of the love of God.
I wish you'd taken me home.
I was lonely and you left me alone to pray for me.
Why didn't you stay?
You seem so holy, so close to God; but I'm still
very hungry, lonely, cold, and still in pain.
Does it matter?

Anonymous

Contentment Is...

Ruth Senter

I heard the voice but couldn't see the person. She was on the other side of the locker, just coming in from her early morning swim. Her voice sounded like the morning itself—bright, cheerful, and full of life. At 6:15 in the morning, it would catch anyone's attention. I heard its affirming tone.

"Delores, I really appreciated the book you picked up for me last week. I know the library was out of your way. I haven't been able to put the book down. Solzhenitsyn is a great writer. I'm glad you suggested him to me."

"Good morning, Pat," she greeted another swimmer. For a moment the melodious voice was silent, then I heard it again. "Have you ever seen such a gorgeous day? I spied a pair of meadowlarks as I walked over this morning. Makes you glad you're alive, doesn't it?"

The voice was too good to be true. Who can be that thankful at this time of the morning? Her voice had a note of refinement to it. Probably some rich woman who has nothing to do all day but sip tea on her verandah and read Solzhenitsyn. I suppose I could be cheerful at 6 A.M. if I could swim and read my way through the day. Probably even owns a cottage in the north woods.

I rounded the corner toward the showers and came face to face with the youthful voice. She was just packing her gear. Her yellow housekeeping uniform hung crisp and neat on her fiftyish frame. It was a uniform I'd seen before—along with mops, brooms, dust cloths, and buckets. An employee of the facility at which I swam. She flashed a smile my way, picked up her plastic K-Mart shopping bag, and hurried out the door, spreading "have a glorious day" benedictions as she went.

I still had the yellow uniform on my mind as I swam my

laps and sank down among the foamy lather of the whirlpool. My two companions were deep in conversation. At least one of them was. His tired, sad voice told tragic woes of arthritic knees, a heart aneurysm, sleepless nights, and pain-filled days.

Nothing was good or right. The water was too hot, the whirlpool jets weren't strong enough for his stiff knees, and his doctors had been much too slow in diagnosing his case. With his diamond-studded hand, he wiped the white suds out of his face. He looked ancient, but I suspected he too was fiftyish.

The yellow uniform and the diamond studded ring stood out in striking, silent contrast, proof to me again that when God says, "Godliness with contentment is great gain," He really means it. This morning I saw both contentment and discontent. I resolved never to forget.

Prayer of St. Francis of Assisi

Lord,
make me an instrument
of Thy peace.
Where there is hatred,
let us sow love;
where there is despair,
hope;
where there is sadness,
joy;
where there is darkness,
light.
O Divine Master,
grant that we may not so much
seek to be consoled,
as to console;
not so much to be loved,
as to love.
For it is in giving that we
receive,
it is in pardoning that we are
pardoned,
it is in dying that we are born again
to eternal life.

Motivation

VISION

An old Chinese proverb

*If your vision is for
a year,
plant wheat.*

*If your vision is for
ten years,
plant trees.*

*If your vision is for
a lifetime
plant people.*

Keeper of the Spring

Charles R. Swindoll

The late Peter Marshall, an eloquent speaker and for several years the chaplain of the United States Senate, used to love to tell the story of "The Keeper of the Spring," a quiet forest dweller who lived high above an Austrian village along the eastern slopes of the Alps. The old gentlemen had been hired many years ago by a young town council to clear away the debris from the pools of water up in the mountain crevices that fed the lovely spring flowing through their town. With faithful, silent regularity, he patrolled the hills, removed the leaves and branches, and wiped away the silt that would otherwise choke and contaminate the fresh flow of water. By and by, the village became a popular attraction for vacationers. Graceful swans floated along the crystal clear spring, the millwheels of various businesses located near the water turned day and night, farmlands were naturally irrigated, and the view from restaurants was picturesque beyond description.

Years passed. One evening the town council met for its semiannual meeting. As they reviewed the budget, one man's eye caught the salary figure being paid the obscure keeper of the spring. Said the keeper of the purse, "Who is the old man? Why do we keep him on year after year? No one ever sees him. For all we know the strange ranger of the hills is doing us no good. He isn't necessary any longer!" By a unanimous vote, they dispensed with the old man's services.

For several weeks nothing changed. By early autumn the trees began to shed their leaves. Small branches snapped off and fell into the pools, hindering the rushing flow of sparkling water. One afternoon someone noticed a slight yellowish-brown tint in the spring. A couple days later the water was

much darker. Within another week, a slimy film covered sections of the water along the banks and a foul odor was soon
detected. The millwheels moved slower, some finally ground
to a halt. Swans left as did the tourists. Clammy fingers of
disease and sickness reached deeply into the village.

Quickly, the embarrassed council called a special meeting.
Realizing their gross error in judgment, they hired back the
old keeper of the spring...and within a few weeks the verita-
ble river of life began to clear up. The wheels started to turn,
and new life returned to the hamlet in the Alps once again.

Fanciful though it may be, the story is more than idle tale.
It carries with it a vivid, relevant analogy directly related to
the times in which we live. What the keeper of the springs
meant to the village, Christian servants mean to our world.
The preserving, taste-giving bite of salt mixed with the
illuminating, hope-giving ray of light may seem feeble and
needless ... but God help any society that attempts to exist
without them! You see, the village without the Keeper of the
Spring is a perfect representation of the world system without
salt and light.

A Man Can't Just Sit Around

Chip McGregor

I suppose most people have dreams, but how many people actually turn their dreams into reality? Larry Walters is among the relatively few who have. His story is true, though you may find it hard to believe.

Larry was a truck driver, but his lifelong dream was to fly. When he graduated from high school, he joined the Air Force in hopes of becoming a pilot. Unfortunately, poor eyesight disqualified him. So when he finally left the service, he had to satisfy himself with watching others fly the fighter jets that crisscrossed the skies over his backyard. As he sat there in his lawn chair, he dreamed about the magic of flying.

Then one day, Larry Walters got an idea. He went down to the local army-navy surplus store and bought a tank of helium and forty-five weather balloons. These were not your brightly colored party balloons, these were heavy-duty spheres measuring more than four feet across when fully inflated.

Back in his yard, Larry used straps to attach the balloons to his lawn chair, the kind you might have in your own backyard. He anchored the chair to the bumper of his jeep and inflated the balloons with helium. Then he packed some sandwiches and drinks and loaded a BB gun, figuring he could pop a few of those balloons when it was time to return to earth.

His preparations complete, Larry Walters sat in his chair and cut the anchoring cord. His plan was to lazily float back down to terra firma. But things didn't quite work out that way.

When Larry cut the cord, he didn't float lazily up; he shot up as if fired from a cannon! Nor did he go up a couple hundred feet. He climbed and climbed until he finally leveled off at eleven thousand feet! At that height, he could hardly risk deflating any of the balloons, lest he unbalance the load and really experience flying! So he stayed up there, sailing around for fourteen hours, totally at a loss as to how to get down.

Eventually, Larry drifted into the approach corridor for Los Angeles International Airport. A Pan Am pilot radioed the tower about passing a guy in a lawn chair at eleven thousand feet with a gun in his lap. (Now there's a conversation I'd have given anything to have heard!)

LAX is right on the ocean, and you may know that at nightfall, the winds on the coast begin to change. So, as dusk fell, Larry began drifting out to sea. At that point, the Navy dispatched a helicopter to rescue him. But the rescue team had a hard time getting to him, because the draft from their propeller kept pushing his home-made contraption farther and farther away. Eventually they were able to hover over him and drop a rescue line with which they gradually hauled him back to earth.

As soon as Larry hit the ground, he was arrested. But as he was being led away in handcuffs, a television reporter called out, "Mr. Walters, why'd you do it?" Larry stopped, eyed the man, then replied nonchalantly, "A man can't just sit around."

Come On, Get with It!

Howard Hendricks

Not long ago I lost one of my best friends, a woman eighty-six years old, the most exciting lay teacher I've ever been exposed to.

The last time I saw her on planet earth was at one of those aseptic Christian parties. We were sitting there on eggshells, looking pious, when she walked in and said, "Well, Hendricks, I haven't seen you for a long time. What are the five best books you've read in the past year?"

She had a way of changing a group's dynamics. Her philosophy was, *Let's not bore each other with each other; let's get into a discussion, and if we can't find anything to discuss, let's get into an argument.*

She was eighty-three on her last trip to the Holy Land. She went there with a group of NFL football players. One of my most vivid memories of her is seeing her out front yelling back to them, "Come on men, get with it!"

She died in her sleep at her daughter's home in Dallas. Her daughter told me that just before she died, she had written out her goals for the next ten years.

May her tribe increase!

The Nearest Battle

Richard C. Halverson
Former Chaplain of the United States Senate

Want to be a winner?

Compete against yourself, not somebody else.

Beating your partner at golf doesn't necessarily mean you shot your best game. Outrunning your rival doesn't mean you ran your best race. You can win over another and still not fulfill your potential.

It's true in all of life. To be your best, you must compete with yourself. It's life's biggest contest.

A loser is a winner—however many his losses—if he conquers himself.

A winner is a loser—however many his victories—if he loses the battle with himself. Alexander the Great conquered the world, and cursed his own lack of self-control.

Victory over others may in fact be the very thing that contributes to the winner's failure to conquer self. Winning makes him proud—arrogant—independent—thoughtless—and sometimes cruel.

To put it another way, it isn't what happens to you that makes the difference, but how you handle it.

The one who stops maturing spiritually because he thinks he knows more Scripture than others or has had more success in ministry, is still far from being what Christ has planned for him.

If you must compare yourself with another, compare yourself with Christ. Let Him mold and fashion your life into the full potential, the divine original He intends.

Mentoring

Chip McGregor

In 1919, a man recovering from injuries suffered in the Great War in Europe rented a small apartment in Chicago. He chose the location for its proximity to the home of Sherwood Anderson, the famous author. Anderson had penned the widely praised novel *Winesburg, Ohio*, and was known for his willingness to help younger writers.

The two men became fast friends and spent nearly every day together for two years. They shared meals, took long walks, and discussed the craft of writing late into the night. The younger man often brought samples of his work to Anderson, and the veteran author responded by giving brutally honest critiques. Yet the young writer was never deterred. Each time, he would listen, take careful notes, and then return to his typewriter to improve his material. He didn't try to defend himself, for, as he put it later, "I didn't know how to write until I met Sherwood Anderson." One of the most helpful things Anderson did for his young protégé was to introduce him to his network of associates in the publishing world. Soon, the younger man was writing on his own. In 1926, he published his first novel, which met with critical acclaim. Its title was *The Sun Also Rises*, and the author's name was Ernest Hemingway.

But wait! The story doesn't end there. After Hemingway left Chicago, Anderson moved to New Orleans. There he met another young wordsmith, a poet with an insatiable drive to improve his skills. Anderson put him through the same paces he had put Hemingway—writing, critiquing, discussing, encouraging—and always more writing. He gave the young man copies of his novels and encouraged him to read them carefully, noting the words, themes, and development of character and story. A year later, Anderson helped this man publish his first novel, *Soldier Pay*. Three years later, this bright new talent, William Faulkner, produced *The Sound and the Fury*, and it quickly became an American masterpiece.

Anderson's role as a mentor to aspiring authors didn't stop there. In California, he spent several years working with playwright Thomas Wolfe and a young man named John Steinbeck, among others. All told, three of Anderson's protégés earned Nobel Prizes and four Pulitzer Prizes for literature. The famous literary critic Malcolm Cowley said that Anderson was "the only writer of his generation to leave his mark on the style and vision of the next generation."

What caused Anderson to so generously give of his time and expertise to help younger people? One reason might be that he himself had sat under the influence of an older writer, the great Theodore Dreiser. He also spent considerable time with Carl Sandburg.

I find this pattern instructive. Not only does it mirror my own experience, it also illustrates what I have found to be a fundamental principle of human experience—that the greatest means of impacting the future is to build into another person's life. This process is called mentoring.

Success

Alice Gray

M other Teresa attended a gathering with kings, and presidents, and statesmen from all over the world. They were there in their crowns and jewels and silks and Mother Theresa wore her sari held together by a safety pin.

One of the noblemen spoke to her of her work with the poorest of the poor in Calcutta. He asked her if she didn't become discouraged because she saw so few successes in her ministry. Mother Theresa answered, "No, I do not become discouraged. You see, God has not called me to a ministry of success. He has called me to a ministry of mercy."

The Red Umbrella

Retold by Tania Gray

As the drought continued for what seemed an eternity, a small community of mid-west farmers were in a quandary as to what to do. The rain was important not only in order to keep the crops healthy, but to sustain the townspeople's very way of living. As the problem became more urgent, the local church felt it was time to get involved and planned a prayer meeting in order to ask for rain.

In what seemed a vague remembrance of an old Native American ritual, the people began to show. The pastor soon arrived and watched as his congregation continued to file in. He slowly circulated from group to group as he made his way to the front in order to officially begin the meeting. Everyone he encountered was visiting across the aisles, enjoying the chance to socialize with their close friends. As the pastor finally secured his place in front of his flock, his thoughts were on the importance of quieting the crowd and starting the meeting.

Just as he began asking for quiet, he noticed an eleven-year-old girl sitting in the front row. She was angelically beaming with excitement and laying next to her was her bright red umbrella, poised for use. The beauty and innocence of this sight made the pastor smile to himself as he realized the faith this young girl possessed that the rest of the people in the room seemed to have forgotten. For the rest had come just to pray for rain...she had come to see God answer.

All It Takes Is a Little Motivation

Zig Ziglar

I love the story the late Dr. Ken McFarland delighted in telling.

It seems a gentleman worked on the 4:00 P.M. to midnight shift, and he always walked home after work. One night the moon was shining so bright he decided to take a shortcut through the cemetery, which would save him roughly a half-mile walk. There were no incidents involved, so he repeated the process on a regular basis, always following the same path. One night as he was walking his route through the cemetery, he did not realize that during the day a grave had been dug in the very center of his path. He stepped right into the grave and immediately started desperately trying to get out. His best efforts failed him, and after a few minutes, he decided to relax and wait until morning when someone would help him out.

He sat down in the corner and was half asleep when a drunk stumbled into the grave. His arrival roused the shift worker since the drunk was desperately trying to climb out, clawing frantically at the sides. Our hero reached out his hand, touched the drunk on the leg, and said, "Friend, you can't get out of here..."—but he did! Now that's motivation!

An Autobiography in Five Short Paragraphs

Portia Nelson

1.

I walk down the street. There is a deep hole in the sidewalk. I fall in. I am lost. I am helpless. It isn't my fault. It takes forever to find a way out.

2.

I walk down the street. There is a deep hole in the sidewalk. I pretend I don't see it. I fall in. I can't believe I'm in the same place, but it isn't my fault. It still takes a long time to get out.

3.

I walk down the street. There is a deep hole in the sidewalk. I see it is there. I still fall in. It's a habit. My eyes are open. I know where I am. It is my fault. I get out immediately.

4.

I walk down the street. There is a deep hole in the sidewalk. I walk around it.

5.

I walk down a different street.

Beautiful Day, Isn't It?

Barbara Johnson

The day started out rotten. I overslept and was late for work. Everything that happened at the office contributed to my nervous frenzy. By the time I reached the bus stop for my homeward trip, my stomach was one big knot.

As usual, the bus was late—and jammed. I had to stand in the aisle. As the lurching vehicle pulled me in all directions, my gloom deepened.

Then I heard a deep voice from up front boom, "Beautiful day, isn't it?" Because of the crowd, I could not see the man, but I could hear him as he continued to comment on the spring scenery, calling attention to each approaching landmark. This church. That park. This cemetery. That firehouse. Soon all the passengers were gazing out the windows. The man's enthusiasm was so contagious I found myself smiling for the first time that day. We reached my stop. Maneuvering toward the door, I got a look at our "guide": a plump figure with a black beard, wearing dark glasses, and carrying a thin white cane.

Don't Give Up . . .

Adapted from a Focus on the
Family Radio Broadcast
Retold by Alice Gray

One day a young man was walking along an isolated road when he heard something like a crying sound. He couldn't tell for sure what the sound was but it seemed to be coming from underneath a bridge. As he approached the bridge, the sound got louder and then he saw a pathetic sight. There, lying in the muddy river bed, was a puppy about two months old. It had a gash on its head and was covered with mud. Its front legs were swollen where they had been tightly bound with cords.

The young man was immediately moved with compassion and wanted to help the dog, but as he approached, the crying stopped and the dog snarled his lip and started to growl. But the young man did not give up. He sat down and started gently talking to the dog. It took a long time but eventually the dog stopped growling and the man was able to inch forward and eventually touch the dog and begin unwrapping the tightly bound cord. The young man carried the dog home, cared for its wounds, gave it food and water and a warm bed. Even with all of this, the dog continued to snarl and growl every time the young man approached. But the young man did not give up.

Weeks went by and the man continued caring for the puppy. Then one day, as the young man approached, the dog wagged its tail. Consistent love and kindness had won and a lifelong friendship of loyalty and trust began.

Let us not become weary in doing good,
for at the proper time we will reap a harvest
if we do not give up.

Galatians 6:9 NIV

Make Up Your Mind, Oreo!

Arthur Gordon

This morning our big cat, Oreo (so named because he is a handsome black-and-white), and I go through a familiar ritual at the back door.

Oreo has been outside for a while and he really wants to come in. So I open the door and wait. But will he come in? No, he won't. He stops and lowers his head suspiciously, as if I were some deadly enemy. "Come on, Oreo," I say impatiently.

He sits down thoughtfully and begins to wash his face with one paw. Maddening.

"Oreo," I say, "I give you food. I supply all your needs. If you do anything in return, I don't know what it is. Now I'm personally inviting you into my house. So come on in!"

Oreo puts one foot across the threshold, then draws it back. He looks out across the yard with some remote, unfathomable expression. He still doesn't come in.

"Oreo," I say, "I'm not going to stand here forever. If you don't come in, I'm going to close this door. This is your last chance!"

I start to close the door slowly. Does he come in? No, he sits there exercising his free will or something. He'll come when it suits him, not before. He figures I'll be patient. So far, he's right.

God made cats. He also made people. I wonder how He feels, sometimes, when He stands at the door and waits...and waits...

I think I know.

Head-Hunter

Josh McDowell

An executive hirer, a "head-hunter" who goes out and hires corporation executives for other firms, once told me, "When I get an executive that I'm trying to hire for someone else, I like to disarm him. I offer him a drink, take my coat off, then my vest, undo my tie, throw up my feet and talk about baseball, football, family, whatever, until he's all relaxed. Then, when I think I've got him relaxed, I lean over, look him square in the eye and say, "What's your purpose in life?" It's amazing how top executives fall apart at that question.

"Well, I was interviewing this fellow the other day, had him all disarmed, with my feet up on his desk, talking about football. Then I leaned up and said, 'What's your purpose in life, Bob?' And he said, without blinking an eye, 'To go to heaven and take as many people with me as I can.' For the first time in my career I was speechless."

If I Had My Life to Live Over

Brother Jeremiah

If I had my life to live over again, I'd try to make more mistakes next time. I would relax. I would limber up. I would be sillier than I have been this trip. I know of a very few things I would take seriously. I would take more trips. I would climb more mountains, swim more rivers and watch more sunsets. I would do more walking and looking. I would eat more ice cream and fewer beans. I would have more actual troubles and fewer imaginary ones. You see, I am one of those people who lives [hygienically] and sensibly and sanely hour after hour, day after day. Oh, I've had my moments; and if I had it to do over again, I'd have more of them. In fact, I'd try to have nothing else. Just moments, one after another, instead of living so many years ahead each day. I have been one of those people who never go anywhere without a thermometer, a hot water bottle, a gargle, a raincoat, aspirin and a parachute. If I had it to do over again, I would go places, do things, and travel lighter than I have.

If I had my life to live over, I would ride on more merry-go-rounds—pick more daisies.

Our Eyes on the Goal

Carole Mayhall

The other night Jack and I watched a television drama called "See How She Runs." The story concerned a 40-year-old divorced teacher from Boston who decided to become a jogger, and eventually entered the 26-mile Boston Marathon. To finish the race became her goal, and in spite of being harassed, jeered at, and assaulted, she did not lose sight of it. The day of the race came and she faced her ultimate test. As she ran, huge blisters developed on her feet. She was also hit and injured by a bicycle. And several miles short of the finish line found her utterly exhausted. Yet she kept going. Then, within a few hundred yards of the finish line, late at night when most other runners had either finished or dropped out, she fell and lay flat on her face, too tired to raise her head. But her friends had put up a crude tape across the finish line and began to cheer her on. She lifted her head with great effort, saw the tape, and realized her goal was within sight. With a supreme effort she got up on her bruised and bleeding feet, and in a burst of energy dredged up from deep inside her courageous heart, she ran the last few yards.

She had kept her eyes on the goal and for the joy of finishing, she endured.

We are to do what our example, Christ, did on earth. He kept looking at the goal, not the going. He was seeing the prize, not the process; the treasure, not the trial; the joy, not the journey. And we must do the same!

Letter to a Coach

An Athlete's Dad

Dear Coach,
I just read your letter to my son and us (the parents) telling of your expectations for athletes under your tutelage. Johnny's mother and I couldn't agree more as we have long recognized the values deriving from high school athletics.

Judging from your record you must teach the game very well. That is important.

There is another phase of coaching, I believe, that is even more important. Permit me to explain what I mean.

Coach, John's mother and I are giving you our most prized possession to use for several weeks. During that time and throughout the next four years our son will make you one of our prime household conversations. He'll tell about how you could have made the Packers if only you hadn't hurt your knee back in '65. He'll tell us about your emotional half-time talk when you came from behind and beat Rivaltown. We'll hear about how you can still pass or kick the football. When we are hearing all this talk our son's eyes will shine. You see, Coach, he'll idolize you.

We don't have many heroes anymore. Joe Willie wears panty-hose! Many professionals would sell their souls for a buck it seems. Some college athletes made the news this year in a very negative manner. We know all college athletes don't shoplift, etc., but that is what we hear about.

You are our son's hero. We are relying on you. His muscles are nearly developed but his mind is still fragile and so impressionable. Your responsibilities are great. Impress him, Coach. Pour it on!

The Greatness of America
Alexander de Tocqueville

Early in the nineteenth century the French statesman, Alexander de Tocqueville, made a study of democracy in our country and wrote as follows...

"I sought for the greatness and genius of America in her commodious harbors and her ample rivers, and it was not there.

"I sought for the greatness and genius of America in her fertile fields and boundless forests, and it was not there.

"I sought for the greatness and genius of America in her rich mines and her vast world commerce, and it was not there.

"I sought for the greatness and genius of America in her public school system and her institutions of learning, and it was not there.

"I sought for the greatness and genius of America in her democratic congress and her matchless constitution, and it was not there.

"Not until I went into the churches of America and heard her pulpits flame with righteousness did I understand the secret of her genius and power.

"America is great because America is good, and if America ever ceases to be good, America will cease to be great."

Bullets or Seeds
Dr. Richard C. Halverson
Former Chaplain of the United States Senate

You can offer your ideas to others as *bullets* or as *seeds*. You can shoot them, or sow them; hit people in the head with them, or plant them in their hearts.

Ideas used as bullets will kill inspiration and neutralize motivation. Used as seeds, they take root, grow, and become reality in the life in which they are planted.

The only risk in the seed approach: Once it grows and becomes part of those in whom it's planted, you probably will get no credit for originating the idea. But if you're willing to do without the credit...you'll reap a rich harvest.

Love

OUTWITTED
Edwin Markham

He drew a circle that shut me out—
Heretic, rebel, a thing to flout.
But Love and I had the wit to win;
We drew a circle that took him in!

The People with the Roses
Max Lucado

John Blanchard stood up from the bench, straightened his
Army uniform and studied the crowd of people making
their way through Grand Central Station. He looked for
the girl whose heart he knew, but whose face he didn't, the
girl with the rose.

His interest in her had begun thirteen months before in a
Florida library. Taking a book off the shelf he found himself
intrigued, not with the words of the book, but with the notes
penciled in the margin. The soft handwriting reflected a
thoughtful soul and insightful mind. In the front of the book,
he discovered the previous owner's name, Miss Hollis
Maynell.

With time and effort, he located her address. She lived in
New York City. He wrote her a letter introducing himself and
inviting her to correspond. The next day he was shipped over-
seas for service in World War II. During the next year and one
month the two grew to know each other through the mail.
Each letter was a seed falling on a fertile heart. A romance
was budding.

Blanchard requested a photograph, but she refused. She
felt that if he really cared, it wouldn't matter what she looked
like.

When the day finally came for him to return from Europe,
they scheduled their first meeting—7:00 P.M. at the Grand
Central in New York. "You'll recognize me," she wrote, "by
the red rose I'll be wearing on my lapel."

So at 7:00 he was in the station looking for a girl whose
heart he loved, but whose face he'd never seen.

I'll let Mr. Blanchard tell you what happened.

A young woman was coming toward me, her figure long and slim. Her blonde hair lay back in curls from her delicate ears; her eyes were as blue as flowers. Her lips and chin had a gentle firmness, and in her pale green suit she was like springtime come alive. I started toward her, entirely forgetting to notice that she was not wearing a rose. As I moved, a small provocative smile turned her lips. "Going my way, sailor?" she murmured.

Almost uncontrollably I made one step closer to her, and then I saw Hollis Maynell.

She was standing almost directly behind the girl. A woman well past 40, she had graying hair tucked under a worn hat. She was more than plump, her thick-ankled feet thrust into low-heeled shoes. The girl in the green suit was quickly walking away. I felt as though I was split in two. So keen was my desire to follow her, and yet so deep was my longing for the woman whose spirit had truly companioned and upheld mine.

And there she stood. Her pale, plump face was gentle and sensible, her gray eyes had a warm and kindly twinkle. I did not hesitate. My fingers gripped the small worn blue leather copy of the book that was to identify me to her. This would not be love, but it would be something precious, something perhaps even better than love, a friendship for which I had been and must ever be grateful.

I squared my shoulders and saluted and held out the book to the woman, even though while I spoke I felt choked by the bitterness of my disappointment. "I'm Lieutenant John Blanchard, and you must be Miss Maynell. I am so glad you could meet me; may I take you to dinner?"

The woman's face broadened into a tolerant smile. "I don't know what this is about, son," she answered, "but the young lady in the green suit who just went by, she begged me to wear this rose on my coat. And she said if you were to ask me out to dinner, I should go and tell you that she is waiting for you in the big restaurant across the street. She said it was some kind of test!" [1]

It's not difficult to understand and admire Miss Maynell's wisdom....

> *"Tell me whom you love,"* Houssaye wrote,
> *"and I will tell you who you are."*

Reflections

Charles R. Swindoll

It happened again last week. As one by one the rest of the family drifted off to bed, I put a couple more logs on the fire, slid into my favorite chair, and read for well over an hour. I came across a few thoughts put together by Ed Dayton, a longtime leader in the World Vision ministry. His words sent me back many, many years when he mentioned watching a short film called *The Giving Tree*, a simple, fanciful piece about a tree that loved a boy.

When the boy was young, he swung from the tree's branches, climbed all over her, ate her apples, slept in her shade. Such happy, carefree days. The tree loved those years.

But as the boy grew, he spent less and less time with the tree. "Come on, let's play," invited the tree on one occasion, but the young man was interested only in money. "Take my apples and sell them" said the tree. He did, and the tree was happy.

He didn't return for a long time, but the tree smiled when he passed one day. "Come on, let's play!" But the man was older and tired of his world. He wanted to get away from it all. "Cut me down. Take my large trunk and make yourself a boat. Then you can sail away," said the tree. The man did, and the tree was happy.

Many seasons passed—summers and winters, windy days and lonely nights—and the tree waited. Finally, the old man returned, too old and tired to play, to pursue riches, or to sail the seas. "I have a pretty good stump left, my friend. Why don't you just sit down here and rest?" said the tree. He did, and the tree was happy.

I stared into the fire, watching my life pass in review as I grew older with the tree and the boy. I identified with both— and it hurt.

How many Giving Trees have there been in my life? How many have released part of themselves so I might grow, accomplish my goals, find wholeness and satisfaction? So, so many. Thank you, Lord, for each one. Their names could fill this page.

The fire died into glowing embers. It was late as I crawled into bed. I had wept, but now I was smiling. "Good night, Lord," I said. I was a thankful man.

Thankful I had taken time to reflect.

The Small Gift

Morris Chalfant
Retold by Marilyn K. McAuley

R ev. Chalfant tells of a couple who were celebrating their golden wedding anniversary. The husband was asked what the secret was to his successful marriage. As the elderly are wont to do, the old gentleman answered with a story.

His wife, Sarah, was the only girl he ever dated. He grew up in an orphanage and worked hard for everything he had. He never had time to date until Sarah swept him off his feet. Before he knew it she had managed to get him to ask her to marry him.

After they had said their vows on their wedding day, Sarah's father took the new groom aside and handed him a small gift. He said, "Within this gift is all you really need to know to have a happy marriage." The nervous young man fumbled with the paper and ribbon until he got the package unwrapped.

Within the box lay a large gold watch. With great care he picked it up. Upon close examination he saw etched across the face of the watch a prudent reminder he would see whenever he checked the time of day...words that, if heeded, held the secret to a successful marriage. They were, "Say something nice to Sarah."

For My Sister

David C. Needham

There is a true story of a little boy whose sister needed a blood transfusion. The doctor explained that she had the same disease the boy had recovered from two years earlier. Her only chance of recovery was a transfusion from someone who had previously conquered the disease. Since the two children had the same rare blood type, the boy was an ideal donor.

"Would you give your blood to Mary?" the doctor asked.

Johnny hesitated. His lower lip started to tremble. Then he smiled and said, "Sure, for my sister."

Soon the two children were wheeled into the hospital room. Mary, pale and thin. Johnny, robust and healthy. Neither spoke, but when their eyes met, Johnny grinned.

As the nurse inserted the needle into his arm, Johnny's smile faded. He watched the blood flow through the tube.

With the ordeal almost over, Johnny's voice, slightly shaky, broke the silence.

"Doctor, *when do I die?*"

Only then did the doctor realize why Johnny had hesitated, why his lip had trembled when he agreed to donate his blood. He thought giving his blood to his sister would mean giving up his life. In that brief moment, he had made his great decision.

Delayed Delivery
Cathy Miller

There had never been such a winter like this. Stella watched from the haven of her armchair as gusts of snow whipped themselves into a frenzy. She feared to stand close to the window, unreasonably afraid that somehow the blizzard might be able to reach her there, sucking her, breathless, out into the chaos. The houses across the street were all but obliterated by the fury of wind-borne flakes. Absently, the elderly woman straightened the slip covers on the arms of her chair, her eyes glued to the spectacle beyond the glass.

Dragging her gaze away from the window, she forced herself up out of her chair and waited a moment for balance to reassert itself. Straightening her back against the pain that threatened to keep her stooped, she set out determinedly for the kitchen.

In the doorway to the next room she paused, her mind blank, wondering what purpose had propelled her there. From the vent above the stove the scream of the wind threatened to funnel the afternoon storm directly down into the tiny house. Stella focused brown eyes on the stovetop clock. The three-fifteen time reminded her that she had headed in there to take something out of the freezer for her supper. Another lonely meal that she didn't feel like preparing, much less eating.

Suddenly, she grabbed the handle of the refrigerator and leaned her forehead against the cold, white surface of the door as a wave of self-pity threatened to drown her. It was too much to bear, losing her beloved Dave this summer! How was she to endure the pain, the daily nothingness? She felt the familiar ache in her throat and squeezed her eyes tightly shut to hold the tears at bay.

Stella drew herself upright and shook her head in silent

chastisement. She reiterated her litany of thanks. She had her health, her tiny home, an income that would suffice for the remainder of her days. She had her books, her television programs, her needlework. There were the pleasures of her garden in the spring and summer, walks through the wilderness park at the end of her street, and the winter birds that brightened the feeders outside her kitchen picture window. Not today though, she thought ruefully, as the blizzard hurled itself against the eastern wall of the kitchen.

"Ah, Dave, I miss you so! I never minded storms when you were here." The sound of her own voice echoed hollowly in the room. She turned on the radio that stood on the counter next to a neatly descending row of wooden canisters. A sudden joyful chorus of Christmas music filled the room, but it only served to deepen her loneliness.

*****

Stella had been prepared for her husband's death. Since the doctor's pronouncement of terminal cancer, they had both faced the inevitable, striving to make the most of their remaining time together. Dave's financial affairs had always been in order. There were no new burdens in her widowed state. It was just the awful aloneness...the lack of purpose to her days.

They had been a childless couple. It had been their choice. Their lives had been so full and rich. They had been content with busy careers, and with each other.

They had many friends. Had. That was the operative word these days. It was bad enough losing the one person you loved with all your heart. But over the past few years, she and Dave repeatedly had to cope with the deaths of their friends and relations. They were all of an age—an age when human bodies began giving up—dying. Face it—they were old!

And now, on the first Christmas without Dave, Stella would be on her own. Mable and Jim had invited her to spend the holiday with them in Florida, but somehow that had seemed worse than staying at home alone. Not only would she miss her husband, but she would miss the snow, and the winter, and the familiarity of her own home.

With shaky fingers, she lowered the volume of the radio so that the music became a muted background. She glanced toward the fridge briefly, then decided that a hot bowl of soup would be more comforting fare this evening.

To her surprise, she saw that the mail had come. She hadn't even heard the creak of the levered mail slot in the front door. Poor mailman, out in this weather! "Neither hail, nor sleet...." With the inevitable wince of pain, she bent to retrieve the damp, white envelopes from the floor. Moving into the living room, she sat on the piano bench to open them. They were mostly Christmas cards, and her sad eyes smiled at the familiarity of the traditional scenes and at the loving messages inside. Carefully, her arthritic fingers arranged them among the others clustered on the piano top. In her entire house, they were the only seasonal decoration. The holiday was less than a week away, but she just did not have the heart to put up a silly tree, or even set up the stable that Dave had built with his own hands.

Suddenly engulfed by the loneliness of it all, Stella buried her lined face in her hands, lowering her elbows to the piano keys in a harsh, abrasive discord, and let the tears come. How would she possibly get through Christmas and the winter beyond it? She longed to climb into bed and bury herself in a cocoon of blankets, not emerging until her friends and spring returned.

The ring of the doorbell echoed the high-pitched, discordant piano notes and was so unexpected that Stella had to stifle a small scream of surprise. Now who could possibly be calling on her on a day like today? Wiping her eyes, she noticed for the first time how dark the room had become. The doorbell sounded a second time.

Using the piano for leverage, she raised herself upright and headed for the front hall, switching on the living room light as she passed. She opened the wooden door and stared through the screened window of the storm door with consternation. On her front porch, buffeted by waves of wind and snow, stood a strange, young man, whose hatless head was barely visible above the large carton in his arms. She peered beyond him to the driveway, but there was nothing about the small car to give clue to his identity. Returning her gaze to him, she saw that his hands were bare and his eyebrows had lifted in an expression of hopeful appeal that was fast disappearing behind the frost forming on the glass. Summoning courage, the elderly lady opened the door slightly and he stepped sideways to speak into the space.

"Mrs. Thornhope?"

She nodded confirmation, her extended arm beginning to tremble with cold and the strain of holding the door against the wind. He continued, predictably, "I have a package for you."

Curiosity drove warning thought from her mind. She pushed the door far enough to enable the stranger to shoulder it and stepped back into the foyer to make room for him. He entered, bringing with him the frozen breath of the storm. Smiling, he placed his burden carefully on the floor and stood to retrieve an envelope that protruded from his pocket. As he handed it to her, a sound came from the box. Stella actually jumped. The man laughed in apology and bent to straighten up the cardboard flaps, holding them open in an invitation for her to peek inside. She advanced cautiously, then turned her gaze downward.

It was a dog! To be more exact, a golden Labrador retriever

puppy. As the gentleman lifted its squirming body up into his arms, he explained, "This is for you, ma'am. He's 6 weeks old and completely housebroken." The young pup wiggled in happiness at being released from captivity and thrust ecstatic, wet kisses in the direction of his benefactor's face. "We were supposed to deliver him on Christmas Eve," he continued with some difficulty, as he strove to rescue his chin from the wet little tongue, "but the staff at the kennels start their holidays tomorrow. Hope you don't mind an early present."

Shock had stolen her ability to think clearly. Unable to form coherent sentences, she stammered, "But...I don't...I mean...who...?"

The young fellow set the animal down on the doormat between them and then reached out a finger to tap the envelope she was still holding.

"There's a letter in there that explains everything, pretty much. The dog was bought last July while her mother was still pregnant. It was meant to be a Christmas gift. If you'll wait just a minute, there are some things in the car I'll get for you."

Before she could protest, he was gone, returning a moment later with a huge box of dog food, a leash, and a book entitled *Caring for Your Labrador Retriever*. All this time the puppy had sat quietly at her feet, panting happily as his brown eyes watched her.

Unbelievably, the stranger was turning to go. Desperation forced the words from her lips. "But who...who bought it?"

Pausing in the open doorway, his words almost snatched away by the wind that tousled his hair, he replied, "Your husband, ma'am." And then he was gone.

*****

It was all in the letter. Forgetting the puppy entirely at this sight of the familiar handwriting, Stella had walked like a somnambulist to her chair by the window. Unaware that the little dog had followed her, she forced her tear-filled eyes to read her husband's words. He had written it three weeks before his death and had left it with the kennel owners to be delivered along with the puppy as his last Christmas gift to her. It was full of love and encouragement and admonishments to be strong. He vowed that he was waiting for the day when she would join him. And he had sent her this young animal to keep her company until then.

Remembering the little creature for the first time, she was surprised to find him quietly looking up at her, his small panting mouth resembling a comic smile. Stella put the pages aside and reached for the bundle of golden fur. She had thought that he would be heavier, but he was only the size and weight of a sofa pillow. And so soft and warm. She cradled him in her arms and he licked her jawbone, then cuddled into the hollow of her neck. The tears began anew at this exchange of affection and the dog endured her crying without moving.

Finally, Stella lowered him to her lap, where she regarded him solemnly. She wiped vaguely at her wet cheeks, then somehow mustered a smile.

"Well, little guy, I guess it's you and me." His pink tongue panted in agreement. Stella's smile strengthened and her gaze shifted sideways to the window. Dusk had fallen, and the storm seemed to have spent the worst of its fury. Through fluffy flakes that were now drifting down to a gentler pace, she saw the cheery Christmas lights that edged the roof lines of her neighbors' homes. The strains of "Joy to the World" wafted in from the kitchen.

Suddenly Stella felt the most amazing sensation of peace and benediction washing over her. It was like being enfolded in a loving embrace. Her heart beat painfully, but it was with joy and wonder, not grief or loneliness. She need never feel alone again. Returning her attention to the dog, she spoke to him. "You know, fella, I have a box in the basement that I think you'd like. There's a tree in it and some decorations and lights that will impress you like crazy! And I think I can find that old stable down there, too. What d'ya say we go hunt it up?" The puppy barked happily in agreement, as if he understood every word.

In the Trenches

Stu Weber

Y ou've probably heard the powerful story coming out of World War I of the deep friendship of two soldiers in the trenches. Two buddies were serving together in the mud and misery of that wretched European stalemate (one version even identifies them as actual brothers). Month after month they lived out their lives in the trenches, in the cold and the mud, under fire and under orders.

From time to time one side or the other would rise up out of the trenches, fling their bodies against the opposing line and slink back to lick their wounds, bury their dead, and wait to do it all over again. In the process, friendships were forged in the misery. Two soldiers became particularly close. Day after day, night after night, terror after terror, they talked of life, of families, of hopes, of what they would do when (and if) they returned from this horror.

On one more fruitless charge, "Jim" fell, severely wounded. His friend, "Bill," made it back to the relative safety of the trenches. Meanwhile Jim lay suffering beneath the night flares. Between the trenches. Alone.

The shelling continued. The danger was at its peak. Between the trenches was no place to be. Still, Bill wished to reach his friend, to comfort him, to offer what encouragement only friends can offer. The officer in charge refused to let Bill leave the trench. It was simply too dangerous. As he turned his back, however, Bill went over the top. Ignoring the smell of cordite in the air, the concussion of incoming rounds, and the pounding in his chest, Bill made it to Jim.

Sometime later he managed to get Jim back to the safety of the trenches. Too late. His friend was gone. The somewhat self-righteous officer, seeing Jim's body, cynically asked Bill if it had been "worth the risk." Bill's response was without hesitation.

"Yes, sir, it was," he said. "My friend's last words made it more than worth it. He looked up at me and said, 'I knew you'd come.'"

GARMENT OF LOVE

Love has a hem to her garment
That reaches the very dust.
It sweeps the streets and lanes,
And because it can, it must.

Mother Teresa

A Crumpled Photograph
Philip Yancey

One holiday I was visiting my mother, who lives seven hundred miles away. We reminisced about times long past, as mothers and sons tend to do. Inevitably, the large box of old photos came down from the closet shelf, spilling out a jumbled pile of thin rectangles that mark my progression through childhood and adolescence: the cowboy-and-Indian getups, the Peter Cottontail suit in the first grade play, my childhood pets, endless piano recitals, the graduations from grade school and high school and finally college.

Among these photos I found one of an infant, with my name written on the back. The portrait itself was not unusual. I looked like any baby: fat-cheeked, half-bald, with a wild, unfocused look to my eyes. But the photo was crumpled and mangled, as if one of those childhood pets had got hold of it. I asked my mother why she had hung onto such an abused photo when she had so many other undamaged ones.

There is something you should know about my family: when I was ten months old, my father contracted spinal lumbar polio. He died three months later, just after my first birthday. My father was totally paralyzed at age twenty-four, his muscles so weakened that he had to live inside a large steel cylinder that did his breathing for him. He had few visitors—people had as much hysteria about polio in 1950 as they do about AIDS today. The one visitor who came faithfully, my mother, would sit in a certain place so that he could see her in a mirror bolted to the side of the iron lung.

My mother explained to me that she kept the photo as a momento, because during my father's illness it had been fastened to his iron lung. He had asked for pictures of her and of his two sons, and my mother had had to jam the pictures in between some metal knobs. Thus, the crumpled condition of my baby photo.

I rarely saw my father after he entered the hospital, since children were not allowed in polio wards. Besides, I was so young that, even if I had been allowed in, I would not now retain those memories.

When my mother told me the story of the crumpled photo, I had a strange and powerful reaction. It seemed odd to imagine someone caring about me whom, in a sense, I had never met.

During the last months of his life, my father had spent his waking hours staring at those three images of his family, my family. There was nothing else in his field of view. What did he do all day? Did he pray for us? Yes, surely. Did he love us? Yes. But how can a paralyzed person express his love, especially when his own children are banned from the room?

I have often thought of that crumpled photo, for it is one of the few links connecting me to the stranger who was my father, a stranger who died a decade younger than I am now. Someone I have no memory of, no sensory knowledge of, spent all day every day thinking of me, devoting himself to me, loving me as well as he could. Perhaps, in some mysterious way, he is doing so now in another dimension. Perhaps I will have time, much time, to renew a relationship that was cruelly ended just as it had begun.

I mention this story because the emotions I felt when my mother showed me the crumpled photo were the very same emotions I felt that February night in a college dorm room when I first believed in a God of love. Someone is there, I realized. Someone is watching life as it unfolds on this planet. More, Someone is there who loves me. It was a startling feeling of wild hope, a feeling so new and overwhelming that it seemed fully worth risking my life on.

Letting Go

Author unknown

To let go doesn't mean to stop caring, it means I can't do it for someone else.

To let go is not to cut myself off, it's the realization that I don't control another.

To let go is not to enable, but to allow learning from natural consequences.

To let go is to admit powerlessness, which means the outcome is not in my hands.

To let go is not to try to change or blame another, I can only change myself.

To let go is not to care for, but to care about.

To let go is not to fix, but to be supportive.

To let go is not to judge, but to allow another to be a human being.

To let go is not to be in the middle arranging all the outcomes, but to allow others to affect their own outcomes.

To let go is not to be protective, it is to permit another to face reality.

To let go is not to deny but to accept.

To let go is not to nag, scold, or argue, but to search out my own shortcomings and to correct them.

To let go is not to adjust everything to my desires but to take each day as it comes and to cherish the moment.

To let go is not to criticize and regulate anyone but to try to become what I dream I can be.

To let go is not to regret the past but to grow and live for the future.

To let go is to fear less and love more.

Love's Power
Alan Loy McGinnis

Viktor Frankl, a Viennese Jew, was interned by the Germans for more than three years. He was moved from one concentration camp to another, even spending several months at Auschwitz. Dr. Frankl said that he learned early that one way to survive was to shave every morning, no matter how sick you were, even if you had to use a piece of broken glass as a razor. For every morning, as the prisoners stood for review, the sickly ones who would not be able to work that day were sent to the gas chambers. If you were shaven, and your face looked ruddier for it, your chances of escaping death that day were better.

Their bodies wasted away on the daily fare of 10 1/2 ounces of bread and 1 3/4 pints of thin gruel. They slept on bare board tiers seven feet wide, nine men to a tier. The nine men shared two blankets together. Three shrill whistles awoke them for work at three A.M.

One morning as they marched out to lay railroad ties in the frozen ground miles from the camp, the accompanying guards kept shouting and driving them with the butts of their rifles. Anyone with sore feet supported himself on his neighbor's arm. The man next to Frankl, hiding his mouth behind his upturned collar, whispered:

"If our wives could see us now! I do hope they are better off in their camps and don't know what is happening to us."

Frankl writes:

That brought thoughts of my own wife to mind. And as we stumbled on for miles, slipping on icy spots, supporting each other time and again, dragging one another up and onward, nothing was said, but we both knew: each of us was thinking of his wife. Occasionally I looked at the sky, where the stars were fading and the pink light of the morning was beginning

to spread behind a dark bank of clouds. But my mind clung to
my wife's image, imagining it with an uncanny acuteness. I
heard her answering me, saw her smile, her frank and encouraging look.

A thought transfixed me: for the first time in my life I saw
the truth as it is set into song by so many poets, proclaimed as
the final wisdom by so many thinkers. The truth—that love is
the ultimate and highest goal to which man can aspire. Then
I grasped the meaning of the greatest secret that human poetry
and human thought and belief have to impart: the salvation of
man is through love and in love.

> *And now these three remain: faith, hope and love.*
> *But the greatest of these is love.*
>   1 *Corinthians 13:13* NIV

The Gift of the Magi

O. Henry

One dollar and eighty-seven cents. That was all. And sixty cents of it was in pennies. Pennies saved one and two at a time by bulldozing the grocer and the vegetable man and the butcher until one's cheeks burned with the silent imputation of parsimony that such close dealing implied. Three times Della counted it. One dollar and eighty-seven cents. And the next day would be Christmas.

There was clearly nothing to do but flop down on the shabby little couch and howl. So Della did. Which instigates the moral reflection that life is made of sobs, sniffles, and smiles, with sniffles predominating.

While the mistress of her home is gradually subsiding from the first stage to the second, take a look at the home. A furnished flat at $8 per week. It did not exactly beggar description, but it certainly had that word on the lookout for the mendicancy squad.

In the vestibule below was a letter-box into which no letter would go, and an electric button from which no mortal finger could coax a ring. Also pertaining thereunto was a card bearing the name, "Mr. James Dillingham Young."

The "Dillingham" had been flung to the breeze during a former period of prosperity when its possessor was being paid $30 per week. Now, when the income was shrunk to $20, the letters of "Dillingham" looked blurred, as though they were thinking seriously of contracting to a modest and unassuming D. But whenever Mr. James Dillingham Young came home and reached his flat above he was called Jim and greatly hugged by Mrs. James Dillingham Young, already introduced to you as Della. Which is all very good.

Della finished her cry and attended to her cheeks with the powder rag. She stood by the window and looked out dully at a gray cat walking a gray fence in a gray backyard. Tomorrow would be Christmas Day, and she had only $1.87 with which to buy Jim a present. She had been saving every penny she could for months, with this result. Twenty dollars a week doesn't go far. Expenses had been greater than she had calculated. They always are. Only $1.87 to buy a present for Jim. Her Jim. Many a happy hour she had spent planning for something nice for him. Something fine and rare and sterling—something just a little bit near to being worthy of the honor of being owned by Jim.

There was a pier-glass between the windows of the room. Perhaps you have seen a pier-glass in an $8 flat. A very thin and very agile person may, by observing his reflection in a rapid sequence of longitudinal strips, obtain a fairly accurate conception of his looks. Della, being slender, had mastered the art.

Suddenly she whirled from the window and stood before the glass. Her eyes were shining brilliantly, but her face had lost its color within twenty seconds. Rapidly she pulled down her hair and let it fall to its full length.

Now, there were two possessions of the James Dillingham Youngs in which they both took a mighty pride. One was Jim's gold watch that had been his father's and his grandfather's. The other was Della's hair. Had the Queen of Sheba lived in the flat across the airshaft, Della would have let her hair hang out the window some day to dry just to deprecate Her Majesty's jewels and gifts. Had King Solomon been the janitor, with all his treasures piled up in the basement, Jim would have pulled out his watch every time he passed, just to see him pluck at his beard from envy.

So now Della's beautiful hair fell around her rippling and shining like a cascade of brown waters. It reached below her knee and made itself almost a garment for her. And then she did it up again nervously and quickly. Once she faltered for a minute and stood still while a tear or two splashed on the worn red carpet.

On went her old brown jacket; on went her old brown hat. With a whirl of skirts and with the brilliant sparkle still in her eyes, she fluttered out the door and down the stairs to the street.

Where she stopped the sign read: "Mme. Sofronie. Hair Goods of All Kinds." One flight up Della ran, and collected herself, panting. Madame, large, too white, chilly, hardly looked the "Sofronie."

"Will you buy my hair?" asked Della.

"I buy hair," said Madame. "Take yer hat off and let's have a sight at the looks of it."

Down rippled the brown cascade.

"Twenty dollars," said Madame, lifting the mass with a practiced hand.

"Give it to me quick," said Della.

Oh, and the next two hours tripped by on rosy wings. Forget the hashed metaphor. She was ransacking the stores for Jim's present.

She found it at last. It surely had been made for Jim and no one else. There was no other like it in any of the stores, and she had turned all of them inside out. It was a platinum fob chain simple and chaste in design, properly proclaiming its value by substance alone and not by meretricious ornamentation—as all good things should do. It was even worthy of The Watch. As soon as she saw it she knew that it must be Jim's. It was like him. Quietness and value—the description applied to both. Twenty-one dollars they took from her for it, and she hurried home with the 87 cents. With that chain on his watch Jim might be properly anxious about the time in any company. Grand as the watch was, he sometimes looked at it on the sly on account of the old leather strap that he used in place of a chain.

When Della reached home her intoxication gave way to prudence and reason. She got out her curling irons and lighted the gas and went to work repairing the ravages made by generosity added to love. Which is always a treacherous task, dear friends—a mammoth task.

Within forty minutes her head was covered with tiny, close-lying curls that made her look wonderfully like a truant schoolboy. She looked at her reflection in the mirror long, carefully, and critically.

"If Jim doesn't kill me," she said to herself, "before he takes a second look at me, he'll say I look like a Coney Island chorus girl. But what could I do—oh! what could I do with a dollar and eighty-seven cents?"

At 7 o'clock the coffee was made and the frying-pan was on the back of the stove and was ready to cook the chops.

Jim was never late. Della doubled the fob chain in her hand and sat on the corner of the table near the door that he always entered. Then she heard his step on the stair away down on the first flight, and she turned white for just a moment. She had a habit of saying little silent prayers about the simplest everyday things, and now she whispered, "Please, God, make him think I am still pretty."

The door opened and Jim stepped in and closed it. He looked thin and very serious. Poor fellow, he was only twenty-two—and to be burdened with a family! He needed a new overcoat and he was without gloves.

Jim stopped inside the door, as immovable as a setter at the scent of a quail. His eyes were fixed upon Della, and there was an expression in them that she could not read, and it terrified her. It was not anger, nor surprise, nor disapproval, nor horror, nor any of the sentiments that she had been prepared for. He simply stared at her fixedly with that peculiar expression on his face.

Della wriggled off the table and went for him.

"Jim, darling," she cried, "don't look at me that way. I had my hair cut off and sold it because I couldn't have lived through Christmas without giving you a present. It'll grow again—you won't mind, will you? I just had to do it. My hair grows awfully fast. Say 'Merry Christmas!' Jim, and let's be happy. You don't know what a nice—what a beautiful, nice gift I've got for you."

"You've cut your hair off?" asked Jim, laboriously, as if he had not arrived at that patent fact yet even after the hardest mental labor.

"Cut it off and sold it," said Della. "Don't you like me just as well, anyhow? I'm me without my hair, ain't I?"

Jim looked around the room curiously.

"You say your hair is gone?" he said, with an air almost of idiocy.

"You needn't look for it," said Della. "It's sold, I tell you— sold and gone, too. It's Christmas Eve, boy. Be good to me, for it went for you. Maybe the hairs of my head were numbered," she went on with a sudden serious sweetness, "but nobody could ever count my love for you. Shall I put the chops on, Jim?"

Out of his trance Jim seemed quickly to wake. He enfolded his Della. For ten seconds let us regard with discreet scrutiny some inconsequential object in the other direction. Eight dollars a week or a million a year—what is the difference? A mathematician or a wit would give you the wrong answer. The magi brought valuable gifts, but that was not among them. This dark assertion will be illuminated later on.

Jim drew a package from his overcoat pocket and threw it upon the table.

"Don't make any mistake, Dell," he said, "about me. I don't think there's anything in the way of a haircut or a shave or a shampoo that could make me like my girl any less. But if you'll unwrap that package you might see why you had me going a while at first."

White fingers and nimble tore at the string and paper. And then an ecstatic scream of joy; and then, alas! a quick feminine change to hysterical tears and wails, necessitating immediate employment of all the comforting powers of the lord of the flat.

For there lay The Combs—the set of combs, side and back, that Della had worshipped for long in a Broadway window. Beautiful combs, pure tortoise shell, with jeweled rims—just a shade to wear in the beautiful vanished hair. They were expensive combs, she knew, and her heart had simply craved and yearned over them without the least hope of possession. And now, they were hers, but the tresses that should have adorned the coveted adornments were gone.

But she hugged them to her bosom, and at length she was able to look up with dim eyes and a smile and say: "My hair grows so fast, Jim!"

And then Della leaped up like a little singed cat and cried, "Oh, oh!"

Jim had not yet seen his beautiful present. She held it out to him eagerly upon her open palm. The dull precious metal seemed to flash with a reflection of her bright and ardent spirit.

"Isn't it a dandy, Jim? I hunted all over town to find it. You'll have to look at the time a hundred times a day now. Give me your watch. I want to see how it looks on it."

Instead of obeying, Jim tumbled down on the couch and put his hands under the back of his head and smiled.

"Dell," said he, "let's put our Christmas presents away and keep 'em a while. They're too nice to use just at present. I sold the watch to get the money to buy your combs. And now suppose you put the chops on."

The magi, as you know, were wise men—wonderfully wise men—who brought gifts to the Babe in the manger. They invented the art of giving Christmas presents. Being wise, their gifts were no doubt wise ones, possibly bearing the privilege of exchange in case of duplication. And here I have lamely related to you the uneventful chronicle of two foolish children in a flat who most unwisely sacrificed for each other the greatest treasures of their house. But in a last word to the wise of these days let it be said that of all who give gifts these two were the wisest. Of all who give and receive gifts, such as they are wisest. Everywhere they are the wisest. They are the magi.

Believing in Each Other

Steve Stephens

L ove believes in all things.

In 1910 DeWitt Wallace developed a new idea for a magazine. It would consist of a collection of condensed articles and he would call it the *Reader's Digest*. He put together a proposed sample and sent it to publishers throughout the country. Nobody seemed interested. DeWitt was terribly discouraged.

About the same time he met Lila Bell Acheson, the daughter of a Presbyterian minister. Before long the two fell in love. Lila believed in DeWitt's dream. She wouldn't let him give up and encouraged him to keep trying his wonderful idea for a magazine. Boosted by her faith in him, DeWitt started mailing circular letters to potential subscribers.

In October, 1921 Lila married DeWitt. On returning from their honeymoon, they found a bundle of letters from interested subscribers. Together they worked on Volume 1, Number 1, which appeared in February, 1922. DeWitt Wallace included Lila Bell Acheson as his co-founder, co-editor, and co-owner. Over the years their little magazine grew. Now printed in at least eighteen languages, *Reader's Digest* is the best selling magazine in the entire world.

DeWitt and Lila were more than husband and wife, they were true friends. They encouraged, supported, and believed in each other. They worked side by side to make their dream come true, and in the process they respected each other. DeWitt once said, "I think Lila made the *Digest* possible." I can imagine that Lila would probably say the same about DeWitt.

Yes, love believes all things. It sticks up for seemingly impossible dreams, cheering as those dreams struggle forward and applauding when they finally come true.

Act of Love

Alice Gray

The story is told of the mother who came home after a long hard day. Her little girl ran out of the house to greet her. "Mommy, Mommy, wait until I tell you what happened today." After listening to a few sentences, the mother responded by indicating the rest could wait as she needed to get dinner started. During the meal, the phone rang, then other family members' stories were longer and louder than the little girl's. Once again she tried after the kitchen was cleaned and the brother's homework questions were answered, but then it was time for her to get ready for bed.

The mom came to tuck her little girl in and quickly listened to her prayers. As she bent down to tousle the little one's curls and to kiss her soft cheek, the child looked up and asked, "Mommy, do you really love me even if you don't have time to listen to me?"

Come Home

Max Lucado

The small house was simple but adequate. It consisted of one large room on a dusty street. Its red-tiled roof was one of many in this poor neighborhood on the outskirts of the Brazilian village. It was a comfortable home. Maria and her daughter, Christina, had done what they could to add color to the gray walls and warmth to the hard dirt floor: an old calendar, a faded photograph of a relative, a wooden crucifix. The furnishings were modest: a pallet on either side of the room, a washbasin, and a wood-burning stove.

Maria's husband had died when Christina was an infant. The young mother, stubbornly refusing opportunities to remarry, got a job and set out to raise her young daughter. And now, fifteen years later, the worst years were over. Though Maria's salary as a maid afforded few luxuries, it was reliable and it did provide food and clothes. And now Christina was old enough to get a job and help out.

Some said Christina got her independence from her mother. She recoiled at the traditional idea of marrying young and raising a family. Not that she couldn't have had her pick of husbands. Her olive skin and brown eyes kept a steady stream of prospects at her door. She had an infectious way of throwing her head back and filling the room with laughter. She also had that rare magic some women have that makes every man feel like a king just by being near them. But it was her spirited curiosity that made her keep all the men at arm's length.

She spoke often of going to the city. She dreamed of trading her dusty neighborhood for exciting avenues and city life. Just the thought of this horrified her mother. Maria was always quick to remind Christina of the harshness of the streets. "People don't know you there. Jobs are scarce and the life is cruel. And besides, if you went there, what would you do for a living?"

Maria knew exactly what Christina would do, or would have to do for a living. That's why her heart broke when she awoke one morning to find her daughter's bed empty. Maria knew immediately where her daughter had gone. She also knew immediately what she must do to find her. She quickly threw some clothes in a bag, gathered up all her money, and ran out of the house.

On her way to the bus stop she entered a drugstore to get one last thing. Pictures. She sat in the photograph booth, closed the curtain, and spent all she could on pictures. With her purse full of small black and white photos, she boarded the next bus to Rio de Janeiro.

Maria knew that Christina had no way of earning money. She also knew that her daughter was too stubborn to give up. When pride meets hunger, a human will do things that were before unthinkable. Knowing this, Maria began her search. Bars, hotels, nightclubs, any place with the reputation for street walkers or prostitutes. She went to them all. And at each place she left her picture—taped to a bathroom mirror, tacked to a hotel bulletin board, fastened to a corner phone booth. And on the back of each photo she wrote a note.

It wasn't too long before both the money and the pictures ran out, and Maria had to go home. The weary mother wept as the bus began its long journey back to her small village.

It was a few weeks later that young Christina descended the hotel stairs. Her young face was tired. Her brown eyes no longer danced with youth but spoke of pain and fear. Her laughter was broken. Her dream had become a nightmare. A thousand times over she had longed to trade these countless beds for her secure pallet. Yet the little village was, in too many ways, too far away.

As she reached the bottom of the stairs, her eyes noticed a

familiar face. She looked again, and there on the lobby mirror was a small picture of her mother. Christina's eyes burned and her throat tightened as she walked across the room and removed the small photo. Written on the back was this compelling invitation. "Whatever you have done, whatever you have become, it doesn't matter. Please come home."

She did.

Family

BLESSED
Theodore Roosevelt, 1917

*No other success in life—not being President,
or being wealthy, or going to college, or writing
a book, or anything else—comes up to the success
of the man or woman who can feel that they have
done their duty and that their children and grandchildren
rise up and call them blessed.*

Someday

Charles R. Swindoll

SOMEDAY WHEN THE KIDS ARE GROWN, things are going to be a lot different. The garage won't be full of bikes, electric train tracks on plywood, sawhorses surrounded by chunks of two-by-fours, nails, a hammer and saw, unfinished "experimental projects," and the rabbit cage. I'll be able to park both cars neatly in just the right places, and never again stumble over skateboards, a pile of papers (saved for the school fund drive), or the bag of rabbit food—now split and spilled.

SOMEDAY WHEN THE KIDS ARE GROWN, the kitchen will be incredibly neat. The sink will be free of sticky dishes, the garbage disposal won't get choked on rubber bands or paper cups, the refrigerator won't be clogged with nine bottles of milk, and we won't lose the tops to jelly jars, catsup bottles, the peanut butter, the margarine, or the mustard. The water jar won't be put back empty, the ice trays won't be left out overnight, the blender won't stand for six hours coated with the remains of a midnight malt, and the honey will stay inside the container.

SOMEDAY WHEN THE KIDS ARE GROWN, my lovely wife will actually have time to get dressed leisurely. A long, hot bath (without three panic interruptions), time to do her nails (even toenails if she pleases!) without answering a dozen questions and reviewing spelling words, having had her hair done that afternoon without trying to squeeze it in between racing a sick dog to the vet and a trip to the orthodontist with a kid in a bad mood because she lost her headgear.

SOMEDAY WHEN THE KIDS ARE GROWN, the instrument called a "telephone" will actually be available. It won't look like it's growing from a teenager's ear. It will simply hang there...silently and amazingly available! It will be free of lipstick, human saliva, mayonnaise, corn chip crumbs, and toothpicks stuck in those little holes.

SOMEDAY WHEN THE KIDS ARE GROWN, I'll be able to see through the car windows. Fingerprints, tongue licks, sneaker footprints and dog tracks (nobody knows how) will be conspicuous by their absence. The back seat won't be a disaster area, we won't sit on jacks or crayons anymore, the tank will not always be somewhere between empty and fumes, and (glory to God!) I won't have to clean up dog messes another time.

SOMEDAY WHEN THE KIDS ARE GROWN, we will return to normal conversations. You know, just plain American talk. "Gross" won't punctuate every sentence seven times. "Yuk!" will not be heard. "Hurry up, I gotta go!" will not accompany the banging of fists on the bathroom door. "It's my turn" won't call for a referee. And a magazine article will be read in full without interruption, then discussed at length without mom and dad having to hide in the attic to finish the conversation.

SOMEDAY WHEN THE KIDS ARE GROWN, we won't run out of toilet tissue. My wife won't lose her keys. We won't forget to shut the refrigerator door. I won't have to dream up new ways of diverting attention from the gumball machine. . . or have to answer "Daddy, is it a sin that you're driving forty-seven in a thirty-mile-per-hour zone?". . .or promise to kiss the rabbit goodnight. . .or wait up forever until they get home from dates. . .or have to take a number to get a word in at the supper table. . .or endure the pious pounding of one Keith Green just below the level of acute pain.

Yes, someday when the kids are grown, things are going to be a lot different. One by one they'll leave our nest, and the place will begin to resemble order and maybe even a touch of elegance. The clink of china and silver will be heard on occasion. The crackling of the fireplace will echo through the hallway. The phone will be strangely silent. The house will be quiet. . .and calm. . .and always clean. . .and empty. . .and we'll spend our time not looking forward to Someday but looking back to Yesterday. And thinking, "Maybe we can baby-sit the grandkids and get some life back in this place for a change!"

"Longer, Daddy, Longer..."

John Trent

R ecently, a woman grabbed my arm at a conference after I had finished speaking on the enormous need we all have for affirmation.

"Dr. Trent, may I tell you my story?" she asked. "Actually, it's a story of something my son did with my granddaughter that illustrates what you've been talking about—the importance of affirmation.

"My son has two daughters, one who's five and one who is in the 'terrible twos'." When a grandmother says this child is in the "terrible twos," believe me, she is!

"For several years, my son has taken the oldest girl out for a 'date' time, but he had never taken the two-year-old until recently. On his first 'date' with the younger one, he took her out to breakfast at a local fast food restaurant.

"They had just gotten their pancakes and my son decided it would be a good time to tell this child how much he loved and appreciated her."

"Jenny," her son had said, "I want you to know how much I love you, and how special you are to Mom and me. We prayed for you for years, and now that you're here and growing up to be such a wonderful girl, we couldn't be more proud of you."

Once he had said all this, he stopped talking and reached over for his fork to begin eating...but he never got the fork to his mouth.

His daughter reached out her little hand and laid it on her father's hand. His eyes went to hers, and in a soft, pleading voice she said, "Longer, Daddy...longer."

He put down his fork and proceeded to tell her some more reasons and ways they loved and appreciated her, and then he again reached for his fork. A second time...and a third...and a fourth time he heard the words, "Longer, Daddy...longer."

This father never did get much to eat that morning, but his daughter got the emotional nourishment she needed so much. In fact, a few days later, she spontaneously ran up to her mother and said, "I'm a really special daughter, Mommy. Daddy told me so."

WISDOM

It's what you learn after you know it all
that counts.

Balloons

James Dobson

S everal weeks ago, I attended a wedding ceremony held in a beautiful garden setting. After the minister instructed the groom to kiss the bride, approximately 150 colorful, helium-filled balloons were released into the blue California sky. It was a pleasant sight that reminded me of a similar moment during the 1984 Olympics in Los Angeles. Within a few seconds, the balloons were scattered across the heavens—some rising hundreds of feet overhead and others cruising toward the horizon. The distribution was curious. They all began from a common launching pad, were filled with approximately the same amount of helium, and ascended into the same conditions of sun and wind. Nevertheless, within a matter of several minutes they were separated by a mile or more. A few balloons struggled to clear the upper branches of trees, while the show-offs became mere pinpoints of color on their journey to the sky. How interesting, I thought—and how symbolic of children.

See footnote and memo in note section in back of the book.

What's a Grandmother?

Letter from a Third Grader

A grandmother is a lady who has no children of her own. She likes other people's little girls and boys. A grandfather is a man grandmother. He goes for walks with the boys, and they talk about fishing and stuff like that.

Grandmothers don't have to do anything except to be there. They're so old that they shouldn't play hard or run. It is enough if they drive us to the market where the pretend horse is, and have lots of dimes ready. Or if they take us for walks, they should slow down past things like pretty leaves and caterpillars. They should never say "hurry up."

Usually, grandmothers are fat, but not too fat to tie your shoes. They wear glasses and funny underwear. They can take their teeth and gums off.

Grandmothers don't have to be smart, only answer questions like, "Why isn't God married?" and "How come dogs chase cats?"

Grandmothers don't talk baby talk like visitors do, because it is hard to understand. When they read to us they don't skip or mind if it is the same story over again.

Everybody should try to have a grandmother, especially if they don't have a television, because they are the only grownups who have time.

The Wall

Author unknown

Their wedding picture mocked them from the table,
these two whose minds no longer touched each
other.

They lived with such a heavy barricade between them
that neither battering ram of words
nor artilleries of touch could break it down.

Somewhere, between the oldest child's first tooth
and the youngest daughter's graduation,
they lost each other.

Throughout the years each slowly unraveled
that tangled ball of string called self,
and as they tugged at stubborn knots,
each hid his searching from the other.

Sometimes she cried at night and
begged the whispering darkness to tell her who she was.
He lay beside her, snoring like a hibernating bear,
unaware of her winter.

Once, after they had made love,
he wanted to tell her how afraid he was of dying,
but, fearful to show his naked soul,
he spoke instead of the beauty of her breasts.

She took a course on modern art,
trying to find herself in colors splashed upon a canvas,
complaining to the other women about men
who are insensitive.

He climbed into a tomb called "The Office,"
wrapped his mind in a shroud of paper figures,
and buried himself in customers.

Slowly, the wall between them rose, cemented by
the mortar of indifference.

One day, reaching out to touch each other,
they found a barrier they could not penetrate,
and recoiling from the coldness of the stone,
each retreated from the stranger on the other side.

For when love dies, it is not in a moment of angry battle,
not when fiery bodies lose their heat.
It lies panting, exhausted
expiring at the bottom of a wall it could not scale.

Soft Touch

James Dobson

My dad was the original soft touch to those who were hungry. He was an evangelist who journeyed from place to place to hold revival meetings. Travel was expensive and we never seemed to have much more money than was absolutely necessary. One of the problems was the way churches paid their ministers in those days. Pastors received a year-round salary but evangelists were paid only when they worked. Therefore, my father's income stopped abruptly during Thanksgiving, Christmas, summer vacation, or any time he rested. Perhaps that's why we were always near the bottom of the barrel when he was at home. But that didn't stop my father from giving.

I remember Dad going off to speak in a tiny church and coming home ten days later. My mother greeted him warmly and asked how the revival had gone. He was always excited about that subject. Eventually, in moments like this she would get around to asking him about the offering. Women have a way of worrying about things like that.

"How much did they pay you?" she asked.

I can still see my father's face as he smiled and looked at the floor. "Aw..." he stammered. My mother stepped back and looked into his eyes.

"Oh, I get it," she said. "You gave the money away again, didn't you?"

"Myrt," he said. "The pastor there is going through a hard time. His kids are so needy. It just broke my heart. They have holes in their shoes and one of them is going to school on these cold mornings without a coat. I felt I should give the entire fifty dollars to them."

My good mother looked intently at him for a moment and then she smiled. "You know, if God told you to do it, it's okay with me."

Then a few days later the inevitable happened. The Dobsons ran completely out of money. There was no reserve to tide us over. That's when my father gathered us in the bedroom for a time of prayer. I remember that day as though it were yesterday. He prayed first.

"Oh Lord, you promised that if we would be faithful with you and your people in our good times, then you would not forget us in our time of need. We have tried to be generous with what you have given us, and now we are calling on you for help."

A very impressionable ten-year-old boy named Jimmy was watching and listening very carefully that day. *What will happen?* he wondered. *Did God hear Dad's prayer?*

The next day an unexpected check for $1200 came for us in the mail. Honestly! That's the way it happened, not just this once but many times. I saw the Lord match my Dad's giving stride for stride. No, God never made us wealthy, but my young faith grew by leaps and bounds. I learned that you cannot outgive God!

My father continued to give generously through the midlife years and into his sixties. I used to worry about how he and Mom would fund their retirement years because they were able to save very little money. If Dad did get many dollars ahead, he'd give them away. I wondered how in the world they would live on the pittance paid to retired ministers by their denomination. (As a widow, my mother received just $80.50 per month after Dad spent forty-four years in the church.) It is disgraceful how poorly we take care of our retired ministers and their widows.

One day my father was lying on the bed and Mom was getting dressed. She turned to look at him and he was crying.

"What's the matter?" she asked.

"The Lord just spoke to me," he replied.

"Do you want to tell me about it?" she prodded.

"He told me something about you," Dad said.

She then demanded that he tell her what the Lord had communicated to him.

My father said, "It was a strange experience. I was just lying here thinking about many things. I wasn't praying or even thinking about you when the Lord spoke to me and said, 'I'm going to take care of Myrtle.'"

Neither of them understood the message, but simply filed it away in the catalog of imponderables. But five days later my dad had a massive heart attack, and three months after that he was gone. At sixty-six years of age, this good man whose name I share went out to meet the Christ whom he had loved and served for all those years.

It was thrilling to witness the way God fulfilled His promise to take care of my mother. Even when she was suffering from end-stage Parkinson's disease and required constant care at an astronomical cost, God provided. The small inheritance that Dad left to his wife multiplied in the years after his departure. It was sufficient to pay for everything she needed, including marvelous and loving care. God was with her in every other way, too, tenderly cradling her in His secure arms until He took her home. In the end, my dad never came close to outgiving God.

When You Thought I Wasn't Looking

Author Unknown

When you thought I wasn't looking, I saw you hang my first painting on the refrigerator, and I wanted to paint another one.

When you thought I wasn't looking, I saw you feed a stray cat, and I thought it was good to be kind to animals.

When you thought I wasn't looking, I saw you make my favorite cake just for me, and I knew that little things are special things.

When you thought I wasn't looking, I heard you say a prayer, and I believed there is a God I could always talk to.

When you thought I wasn't looking, I felt you kiss me goodnight, and I felt loved.

When you thought I wasn't looking, I saw tears come from your eyes, and I learned that sometimes things hurt, but it's all right to cry.

When you thought I wasn't looking, I saw that you cared, and I wanted to be everything that I could be.

When you thought I wasn't looking, I looked...and wanted to say thanks for all the things I saw when you thought I wasn't looking.

Growing Up
Marilyn K. McAuley

Danny was only three when he and his daddy came to live with us for a year. Every morning we would stand at the door and throw kisses and wave good-bye as Grandpa and Daddy left for their jobs. Then Danny and Grandma would get the house in order so we could build skyscrapers with building blocks and journey into wonderful places reading book after book. Later we would walk our country lane out to the highway to get the mail each day and listen to the wind whisper through the tall fir trees.

After work one evening, Grandpa swung Danny in the air and said, "Let's go get a hamburger." As we drove three-quarters of an hour to town we sang and talked and then it grew quiet. Danny was thinking. He said, "Grandpa has a job and Daddy has a job and when I grow up, I'll have a job."

"That's right Danny," said Grandpa.

After a little more thought, Danny added, "And when Grandma grows up she'll get a job too."

Even If It's Dark

Ron Mehl

He was a strong man facing an enemy beyond his strength.

His young wife had become gravely ill, then suddenly passed away, leaving the big man alone with a wide-eyed, flax-en-haired girl, not quite five years old.

The service in the village chapel was simple, and heavy with grief. After the burial at the small cemetery, the man's neighbors gathered around him. "Please, bring your little girl and stay with us for several days," someone said. "You shouldn't go back home just yet."

Broken-hearted though he was, the man answered, "Thank you, friends, for the kind offer. But we need to go back home—where she was. My baby and I must face this."

So they returned, the big man and his little girl, to what now seemed an empty, lifeless house. The man brought his daughter's little bed into his room, so they could face the first dark night together.

As the minutes slipped by that night, the young girl was having a dreadful time trying to sleep...and so was her father. What could pierce a man's heart deeper than a child sobbing for a mother who would never come back?

Long into the night the little one continued to weep. The big man reached down into her bed and tried to comfort her as best he could. After a while, the little girl managed to stop crying—but only out of sorrow for her father. Thinking his daughter was asleep, the father looked up and said brokenly, "I trust You, Father, but...it's as dark as midnight!"

Hearing her dad's prayer, the little girl began to cry again.

"I thought you were asleep, baby," he said.

"Papa, I did try. I was sorry for you. I did try. But—I couldn't go to sleep. Papa, did you ever know it could be so dark? Why Papa? I can't even see you, it's so dark." Then, through her tears, the little girl whispered, "But you love me even if it's dark—don't you, Papa? You love me even if I don't see you, don't you, Papa?"

For an answer, the big man reached across with his massive hands, lifted his little girl out of her bed, brought her over onto his chest, and held her, until at last she fell asleep.

When she was finally quiet, he began to pray. He took his little daughter's cry to him, and passed it up to God.

"Father, it's dark as midnight. I can't see You at all. But You love me, even when it's dark and I can't see, don't You?"

From that blackest of hours, the Lord touched him with new strength, enabling him to carry on. He knew that God went on loving him, even in the dark.

Got a Minute?

David Jeremiah

A mother who had just finished reading a book on parenting...was convicted about some of the things she had been failing to do as a parent. Feeling this conviction, she went upstairs to talk to her son. When she got upstairs, all she could hear coming from her boy's room was the loud sound of his drums. She had a message she wanted to deliver, but when she knocked on the door, she got cold feet.

"Got a minute?" she said, as her son answered her knock. "Mom, you know I always have a minute for you," said the boy.

"You know, son, I...I...I just love the way you play the drums."

He said, "You do? Well, thanks Mom!"

She got up and started back downstairs. Half-way down, she realized that she had not conveyed the message she had intended so back she went to his door and once again knocked. "It's Mom again! Do you have another minute?" she said.

He said, "Mom, like I told you before, I always have a minute for you."

She went over and sat on the bed. "When I was here before I had something I wanted to tell you and I didn't get it said. What I really meant to say was...your dad and I...we just really think you're great."

He said, "You and Dad?"

She said, "Yes, your Dad and I."

"Okay, Mom. Thanks a lot."

She left and was once again half-way down the stairs when she realized she had gotten closer to the message she intended but had still not told her boy that she loved him. So up the stairs again and back to the door again, and this time he heard her coming. Before she could ask he shouted, "Yeah, I have a minute!"

Mom sat down on the bed once more. "You know, Son, I've tried this twice now and haven't gotten it out. What I really came up here to tell you is this. I love you. I love you with all my heart. Not Dad and I love you, but I love you."

He said, "Mom, that's great. I love you, too!" He gave her a great big hug.

She started out of the room and was back at the head of the stairs when her son stuck his head out of his room and said, "Mom, do you have a minute?"

She laughed and said, "Sure."

"Mom," he said, "did you just come back from a seminar?"

A Father's Prayer of Enlightenment

John Ellis

Dear Heavenly Father, can you forgive me for hurting my children?

I came from a poor background so I thought that a big house would make my children feel important. I didn't realize that all it takes is my love.

I thought money would bring them happiness, but all it did was make them think that things were more important than people.

I thought spanking them would make them tough so that they could defend themselves. All it did was stop me from seeking wisdom so that I could discipline and teach them.

I thought that leaving them alone would make them independent. All it did was force my one son to be the father to my second son.

I thought that by smoothing over all of the family problems I was keeping peace. All I was teaching them was to run rather than lead.

I thought that by pretending to be the perfect family in public that I was bringing them respectability. All I was teaching them was to live a lie and keep the secret.

I thought that all I had to do to be a father was make money, stay at home and supply all their material needs. All I taught them was that there is more to being a dad. The problem is they will have to guess what being a dad really is.

And Dear God,

I hope you can read this prayer. My tears have smudged a lot of words.

Summer Vacation

Bruce Larson

I have a great friend down in Montgomery, Alabama, and a few years ago he told me an unforgettable story of a summer vacation he had planned for his wife and children. He was unable to go because of business, but he helped them plan every day of a camping trip in the family station wagon from Montgomery all the way to California, up the West Coast, and then back to Montgomery.

He knew their route exactly and the precise time they would be crossing the Great Divide. So, my friend arranged to fly himself out to the nearest airport and hire a car and a driver to take him to a place which every car must pass. He sat by the side of the road several hours waiting for the sight of that familiar station wagon. When it came into view, he stepped out in the road and put his thumb out to hitchhike a ride with the family who assumed that he was 3,000 miles away.

I said to him, "Coleman, I'm surprised they didn't drive off the road in terror or drop dead of a heart attack. What an incredible story. Why did you go to all that trouble?"

"Well, Bruce," he said, "someday I'm going to be dead, and when that happens, I want my kids and my wife to say, 'You know, Dad was a lot of fun.'"

Wow, I thought. *Here's a man whose whole game plan is to make fun and happiness for other people.* It made me wonder what my own family will remember about me. I'm sure they will say, "Well dad was a nice guy but he sure worried a lot about putting out the lights and closing the windows and picking up around the house and cutting the grass." But I'd also like them to be able to say that Dad was the guy who made life a lot of fun.

To My Grown-Up Son
Author Unknown

My hands were busy through the day;
I didn't have much time to play
The little games you asked me to—
I didn't have much time for you.
I'd wash your clothes, I'd sew and cook;
But when you'd bring your picture book
And ask me please to share your fun,
I'd say: "A little later, son."

I'd tuck you in all safe at night,
And hear your prayers, turn out the light,
Then tip-toe softly to the door....
I wish I'd stayed a minute more.

For life is short, the years rush past....
A little boy grows up so fast.
No longer is he at your side,
His precious secrets to confide.
The picture books are put away;
There are no longer games to play.
No good-night kiss, no prayers to hear—
That all belongs to yesteryear.

My hands, once busy, now are still.
The days are long and hard to fill.
I wish I could go back and do
The little things you asked me to.

Christmas Day in the Morning

Pearl S. Buck

He waked suddenly and completely. It was four o'clock, the hour at which his father had always called him to get up and help with the milking. Strange how the habits of his youth clung to him still! Fifty years ago, and his father had been dead for thirty years, and yet he waked at four o'clock in the morning. He had trained himself to turn over and go to sleep, but this morning, because it was Christmas, he did not try to sleep.

He slipped back in time, as he did so easily nowadays. He was fifteen years old and still on his father's farm. He loved his father. He had not known it until one day a few days before Christmas, when he overheard what his father was saying to his mother.

"Mary, I hate to call Rob in the mornings. He's growing so fast, and he needs his sleep. If you could see how he sleeps when I go in to wake him up! I wish I could manage alone."

"Well, you can't, Adam." His mother's voice was brisk. "Besides, he isn't a child anymore. It's time he took his turn."

"Yes," his father said slowly. "But I sure do hate to wake him."

When he heard those words, something in him woke: his father loved him! He had never thought of it before, taking for granted the tie of their blood. Neither his father nor his mother talked about loving their children—they had no time for such things. There was always so much to do on a farm.

Now that he knew his father loved him, there would be no more loitering in the mornings and having to be called again. He got up after that, stumbling with sleep, and pulled on his clothes, his eyes shut, but he got up.

And then on the night before Christmas, that year when he was fifteen, he lay for a few minutes thinking about the next day. They were poor, and most of the excitement was in the turkey they had raised themselves and in the mince pies his mother made. His sisters sewed presents and his mother and father always bought something he needed, not only a warm jacket, maybe, but something more, such as a book. And he saved and bought them each something, too.

He wished, that Christmas he was fifteen, he had a better present for his father. As usual, he had gone to the ten-cent store and bought a tie. It had seemed nice enough until he lay thinking the night before Christmas, and then he wished that he had heard his father and mother talking in time for him to save for something better.

He lay on his side, his head supported by his elbow, and looked out of his attic window. The stars were bright, much brighter than he ever remembered them being, and one was so bright he wondered if it were really the star of Bethlehem.

"Dad," he had once asked when he was a little boy, "what is a stable?"

"It's just a barn," his father had replied, "like ours."

Then Jesus had been born in a barn, and to a barn the shepherds and the Wise Men had come, bringing their Christmas gifts!

The thought struck him like a silver dagger. Why should he not give his father a special gift, too, out there in the barn? He could get up early, earlier than four o'clock, and he could creep into the barn and get all the milking done. He'd do it alone, milk and clean up, and then when his father went in to start the milking, he'd see it all done. And he would know who had done it.

At a quarter to three, he got up and put on his clothes. He crept downstairs, careful of the creaky boards, and let himself out. The big star hung lower over the barn roof, a reddish gold. The cows looked at him, sleepy and surprised.

"So, boss," he whispered. They accepted him placidly, and he fetched some hay for each cow and then got the milking pail and the big milk cans.

He had never milked all alone before, but it seemed almost easy. He kept thinking about his father's surprise. His father would come in and call him, saying that he would get things started while Rob was getting dressed. He'd go to the barn, open the door, and then he'd go to get the two big empty milk cans. But they wouldn't be waiting or empty; they'd be standing in the milkhouse, filled.

The task went more easily than he had ever known it to before. Milking for once was not a chore. It was something else, a gift to his father who loved him. He finished, the two milk cans were full, and he covered them and closed the milk-house door carefully, making sure of the latch. He put the stool in its place by the door and hung up the clean milk pail. Then he went out of the barn and barred the door behind him.

Back in his room, he had only a minute to pull off his clothes in the darkness and jump into bed, for he heard his father up. He put the covers over his head to silence his quick breathing. The door opened.

"Rob!" his father called. "We have to get up, son, even if it is Christmas."

"Aw-right," he said sleepily.

"I'll go on out," his father said. "I'll get things started."

The door closed and he lay still, laughing to himself. In just a few minutes his father would know. His dancing heart was ready to jump from his body.

The minutes were endless—ten, fifteen, he did not know how many—and he heard his father's steps again. The door opened and he lay still.

"Rob!"

"Yes, Dad—"

His father was laughing, a queer sobbing sort of laugh. "Thought you'd fool me, did you?" His father was standing beside him, pulling away the cover.

"It's for Christmas, Dad!"

He found his father and clutched him in a great hug. He felt his father's arms go around him. It was dark, and they could not see each other's faces.

"Son, I thank you. Nobody ever did a nicer thing—"

"Oh, Dad, I want you to know—I do want to be good!" The words broke from him of their own will. He did not know what to say. His heart was bursting with love.

"Well, I reckon I can go back to bed and sleep," his father said after a moment. "No, hark—the little ones are waked up. Come to think of it, son, I've never seen you children when you first saw the Christmas tree. I was always in the barn. Come on!"

Rob got up and pulled on his clothes again, and they went down to the Christmas tree; and soon the sun was creeping up where the star had been. Oh, what a Christmas, and how his heart had nearly burst again with shyness and pride as his father told his mother and made the younger children listen about how he, Rob, had gotten up all by himself.

"The best Christmas gift I ever had, and I'll remember it, son, every year on Christmas morning, so long as I live."

They both remembered it, and now that his father was dead he remembered it alone: that blessed Christmas dawn when, alone with the cows in the barn, he had made his first gift of true love.

27 Things Not to Say to Your Spouse

Steve Stephens

There is nothing more painful than having unhealthy communication with the one you love. It is through communication that we connect and our spirits touch. If that connection becomes contaminated, it is only a matter of time before the whole relationship is poisoned. In the process of communication, wisdom is knowing what not to say rather than what to say....

Therefore, I gathered together some close friends and asked them what not to say to your spouse. Here is their list:

"I told you so."
"You're just like your mother."
"You're always in a bad mood."
"You just don't think."
"It's your fault."
"What's wrong with you?"
"All you ever do is complain."
"I can't do anything to please you."
"You get what you deserve."
"Why don't you ever listen to me?"
"Can't you be more responsible?"
"What were you thinking?"
"You're impossible!"
"I don't know why I put up with you."
"I can talk to you until I'm blue in the face and it doesn't do any good."
"I can do whatever I like."
"If you don't like it, you can just leave."
"Can't you do anything right?"

"That was stupid."
"All you ever do is think of yourself."
"If you really loved me, you'd do this."
"You're such a baby."
"Turnabout's fair play."
"You deserve a dose of your own medicine."
"What's your problem?"
"I can never understand you."
"Do you always have to be right?"

37 Things to Say to Your Spouse

Steve Stephens

A healthy marriage is a safe haven where we can relax and recuperate from the tensions of everyday life. We need to hear positive things from our mate. Just as I gathered together some friends to tell me what not to say to a spouse, so they also suggested what they would like to hear from their spouse.

"Good job!"

"You are wonderful."

"That was really great."

"You look gorgeous today."

"I don't feel complete without you."

"I appreciate all the things you've done for me all these years."

"You come first in my life, before kids, career, friends, anything."

"I'm glad I married you."

"You're the best friend I have."

"If I had to do it over again, I'd still marry you."

"I wanted you today."

"I missed you today."

"I couldn't get you out of my mind today."

"It's nice to wake up next to you."

"I will always love you."

"I love to see your eyes sparkle when you smile."

"As always, you look good today."

"I trust you."

"I can always count on you."

"You make me feel good."

"I'm so proud to be married to you."
"I'm sorry."
"I was wrong."
"What would you like?"
"What is on your mind?"
"Let me just listen."
"You are so special."
"I can't imagine life without you."
"I wish I were a better partner."
"What can I do to help?"
"Pray for me."
"I'm praying for you today."
"I prize every moment we spend together."
"Thank you for loving me."
"Thank you for accepting me."
"Thank you for being my partner."
"You make every day brighter."

Of More Value

Jerry B. Jenkins

A friend, the father of two daughters, admits he doesn't mind putting a little fear into the boys. His daughters may be embarrassed when he asks for a few moments alone with their dates, and he might rather the young men think he's an okay guy than that he's a mean, protective father. But some things are worth a little awkwardness. Boys might think such dads are a little overprotective. To the fathers of daughters, however, there is no such thing as over-protective.

Another friend says he uses a sports-car analogy to get his point across. He'll say to the boy, "If I owned the most expensive, exotic sports car on the road and I let you take it for a spin, you'd be careful with it, wouldn't you?"

"Oh, yes, sir, you bet."

"You'd treat it better than if it was your own, wouldn't you?"

"Yes, sir."

"I wouldn't want to think you were screeching the tires, would I?"

"No, sir."

"Well, let me tell you something, just so we're straight with each other, man to man. My daughter is of infinitely more value to me than any car could be. Do you get my drift? She's on loan from me to you for the next few hours, and I wouldn't want to discover that she was treated with any less care or respect than I would give her. I'm responsible for her. She's mine. I'm entrusting her to you. That trust brooks no second chances. Understand?"

By then, of course, the young man is wondering why he didn't ask someone else out. He's only nodding, unable to speak. Most often, he brings the girl home earlier than

promised. The daughter might even complain about her
father's approach, but deep down she feels loved and cherished, and you can be sure she'll marry a man who treats her
that way.

TESTAMENT
Patrick Henry

I have now disposed of all my property to my family.
There is one thing more I wish I could give them, and
that is the Christian religion. If they had that, and I
had not given them one shilling, they would have been
rich, and if they had not that, and I had given them all
the world, they would be poor.

A Son of Such Tears

Ruth Bell Graham
Retold by Casandra Lindell

Saint Augustine did not start out that way. His mother, Monica, taught him about Christianity carefully and she prayed, but his incredible mind had always troubled her. One day, in his teenage years, he announced that he was throwing aside her faith in Christ to follow current heresies![1] He went on to live a life of immorality. And Augustine never did anything by halves. He was the best and the first in school, and he became the best and first in the vulgar festivities of youth.

I could not distinguish between the clear shining of affection and the darkness of lust....I could not keep within the kingdom of light, where friendship binds soul to soul....And so I polluted the brook of friendship with the sewage of lust.[2]

I was grown deaf by the clanking of the chain of my mortality, the punishment of the pride of my soul, and I strayed further from You, and You left me alone, and I was tossed about, and wasted, and dissipated, and I boiled over in my fornications, and You held Your peace, O Thou my tardy joy!...[3]

Each of us sins in his own way. Some of us allow ourselves to be deceived because our sin is socially acceptable; we reason that it really isn't that bad after all. Some of us suffer consequences because our sin is not acceptable in our society; we may end up in jail or ignored by the people who used to call us friend. But Augustine's story is still our own:

The loss of faith always occurs when the senses first awaken. At this critical moment, when nature claims us for her service, the consciousness of spiritual things is, in most cases, either eclipsed or totally destroyed. *It is not reason which turns the young man from God; it is the flesh.* Skepticism but provides him with the excuses for the new life he is leading.[4]

Still, Monica prayed. She prayed through her son's sin and she prayed through her son's heresy. She prayed her son through his fight with God. And Augustine knew it.

Almost nine years passed, in which I wallowed in the mire of that deep pit, and the darkness of falsehood....All which time that chaste, godly and sober widow...ceased not at all hours of her devotions to bewail my case unto You. And her prayers entered into Your presence; and yet You [allowed] me to be yet involved and reinvolved in that darkness.[5]

Those years were not easy for Monica, as any mother of a child lost in darkness knows. Those years hurt. Finally, she went to the bishop, a devout man who knew the Scriptures inside and out, and asked him to talk to Augustine, to refute his errors. The bishop refused—Augustine had quite a reputation as an orator and debater by then.

Instead, he wisely comforted Monica by saying that a mind so sharp would eventually see through the deception. He offered himself as an example—he had once been a Manichaean.

Monica would not be consoled by those words. She continued to beg the bishop, and plead with him through rivers of tears. Finally, wearied by her tenacity but at the same time moved by the ache in her soul for her son, the bishop said, "Go, go! Leave me alone. Live on as you are living. It is not possible that the son of such tears should be lost." Harshness interwoven with kindness and compassion.

The son of such tears continued to run from his mother and from his God. He ran for many more years. Then, one day, Augustine listened to Saint Ambrose, bishop of Milan and the most eminent churchman of the day. Exhausted by the years of running, convicted and broken, he turned to embrace Jesus.

Saint Augustine changed the course of history, according to Christian historians and scholars. His works have been more widely read than almost any other author's throughout the centuries; he can also speak to the present generation as one heart speaks to another. Saint Augustine more than fulfilled his godly mother's prayers and hopes. Some credit him as God's tool that kept the light of the New Testament shining when the Roman Empire fell apart.[6]

Not too long after her prodigal Augustine came home for good, she told him that she had nothing left to live for. Her lifelong quest had been to see him come back to Jesus. Nine days later, she was dead.

The father of the Prodigal Son in the Book of Luke was so focused on seeing his son return that he spotted him when he was "still a great way off." Monica did the same. She followed him where he ran; she challenged his rebellious ways when he came home. She never stopped praying for her son of such tears.

Augustine learned from her what so many prodigals have learned about our heavenly Father: "The only way a man can lose You is to leave You; and if he leaves You, where does he go? He can only run from Your pleasure to Your wrath."[7]

It is the deepest desire of our God to move people from being the focus of His wrath to the delight of His heart. It is unspeakably hard to watch a son or daughter find his or her own way, but that is what each of us must do. Jesus would have it no other way. Hope for them, pray for them, and never stop crying for them. And then look up the road expectantly, your son of such tears just might be standing out clearly on the dusty horizon.

See footnotes and memo in note section in back of the book.

A Family for Freddie

Abbie Blair
*Reprinted with permission from the
December 1964 Reader's Digest*

I remember the first time I saw Freddie. He was standing in his playpen at the adoption agency where I work. He gave me a toothy grin. "What a beautiful baby," I thought.

His boarding mother gathered him into her arms. "Will you be able to find a family for Freddie?"

Then I saw it. Freddie had been born without arms.

"He's so smart. He's only ten months old, and already he walks and talks." She kissed him. "Say 'book' for Mrs. Blair."

Freddie grinned at me and hid his head on his boarding mother's shoulder. "Now, Freddie, don't act that way," she said. "He's really very friendly," she added. "Such a good, good boy."

Freddie reminded me of my own son when he was that age, the same thick dark curls, the same brown eyes.

"You won't forget him, Mrs. Blair? You will try?"

"I won't forget."

I went upstairs and got out my latest copy of the Hard-to-Place list.

Freddie is a ten-month-old white Protestant boy of English and French background. He has brown eyes, dark-brown hair and fair skin. Freddie was born without arms, but is otherwise in good health. His boarding mother feels he is showing signs of superior mentality, and he is already walking and saying a few words. Freddie is a warm, affectionate child who has been surrendered by his natural mother and is ready for adoption.

"He's ready," I thought. "But who is ready for him?"

It was ten o'clock of a lovely late-summer morning, and the agency was full of couples—couples having interviews, couples meeting babies, families being born. These couples nearly always have the same dream: they want a child as much like themselves as possible, as young as possible, and—most important—a child with no medical problem.

"If he develops a problem after we get him," they say, "that is a risk we'll take, just like any other parents. But to pick a baby who already has a problem—that's too much."

And who can blame them?

I wasn't alone in looking for parents for Freddie. Any of the caseworkers meeting a new couple started with a hope: maybe they were for Freddie. But summer slipped into fall, and Freddie was with us for his first birthday.

"Freddie is so-o-o big," said Freddie, laughing. "So-o-o big."

And then I found them.

It started out as it always does—an impersonal record in my box, a new case, a new "Home Study," two people who wanted a child. They were Frances and Edwin Pearson. She was 41. He was 45. She was a housewife. He was a truck driver.

I went to see them. They lived in a tiny white frame house in a big yard full of sun and old trees. They greeted me together at the door, eager and scared to death.

Mrs. Pearson produced steaming coffee and oven-warm cookies. They sat before me on the sofa, close together, holding hands. After a moment, Mrs. Pearson began: "Today is our wedding anniversary. Eighteen years."

"Good years." Mr. Pearson looked at his wife. "Except—"

"Yes," she said. "Except. Always the 'except.'" She looked around the immaculate room. "It's too neat," she said. "You know?"

I thought of my own living room with my three children. Teen-agers now. "Yes," I said. "I know."

"Perhaps we're too old?"

I smiled. "You don't think so," I said. "We don't either."

"You always think it will be this month, and then next

month," Mr. Pearson said. "Examinations. Tests. All kinds of things. Over and over. But nothing ever happened. You just go on hoping and hoping, and time keeps slipping by."

"We've tried to adopt before this," Mr. Pearson said. "One agency told us our apartment was too small, so we got this house. Then another agency said I didn't make enough money. We had decided that was it, but this friend told us about you, and we decided to make one last try."

"I'm glad," I said.

Mrs. Pearson glanced at her husband proudly. "Can we choose at all?" she asked. "A boy for my husband?"

"We'll try for a boy," I said. "What kind of boy?"

Mrs. Pearson laughed. "How many kinds are there? Just a boy. My husband is very athletic. He played football in high school; basketball, too, and track. He would be good for a boy."

Mr. Pearson looked at me. "I know you can't tell exactly," he said, "but can you give us any idea how soon? We've waited so long."

I hesitated. There is always this question.

"Next summer maybe," said Mrs. Pearson. "We could take him to the beach."

"That long?" Mr. Pearson said. "Don't you have anyone at all? There must be a little boy somewhere."

"Of course," he went on after a pause, "we can't give him as much as other people. We haven't a lot of money saved up."

"We've got a lot of love," his wife said. "We've saved up a lot of that."

"Well," I said cautiously, "there is a little boy. He is 13 months old."

"Oh," Mrs. Pearson said, "just a beautiful age."

"I have a picture of him," I said, reaching for my purse. I handed them Freddie's picture.

"He is a wonderful little boy," I said. "But he was born

without arms."

They studied the picture in silence. He looked at her. "What do you think, Fran?"

"Kickball," Mrs. Pearson said. "You could teach him kickball."

"Athletics are not so important," Mr. Pearson said. "He can learn to use his head. Arms he can do without. A head, never. He can go to college. We'll save for it."

"A boy is a boy," Mrs. Pearson insisted. "He needs to play. You can teach him."

"I'll teach him. Arms aren't everything. Maybe we can get him some."

They had forgotten me. But maybe Mr. Pearson was right, I thought. Maybe sometime Freddie could be fitted with artificial arms. He did have nubs where arms should be.

"Then you might like to see him?"

They looked up. "When could we have him?"

"You think you might want him?"

Mrs. Pearson looked at me. "Might?" she said. "Might?"

"We want him," her husband said.

Mrs. Pearson went back to the picture. "You've been waiting for us," she said. "Haven't you?"

"His name is Freddie," I said, "but you can change it."

"No," said Mr. Pearson. "Frederick Pearson—it's good together."

And that was it.

There were formalities, of course; and by the time we set the day Christmas lights were strung across city streets and wreaths were hung everywhere.

I met the Pearsons in the waiting room. There was a little snow on them both.

"Your son's here already," I told them. "Let's go upstairs and I'll bring him to you."

"I've got butterflies," Mrs. Pearson announced. "Suppose

he doesn't like us?"

I put my hand on her arm. "I'll get him," I said.

Freddie's boarding mother had dressed him in a new white suit, with a sprig of green holly and red berries embroidered on the collar. His hair shone, a mop of dark curls.

"Going home," Freddie said to me, smiling, as his boarding mother put him in my arms.

"I told him that," she said. "I told him he was going to his new home."

She kissed him, and her eyes were wet.

"Good-bye, dear. Be a good boy."

"Good boy," said Freddie cheerfully. "Going home."

I carried him upstairs to the little room where the Pearsons were waiting. When I got there, I put him on his feet and opened the door.

"Merry Christmas," I said.

Freddie stood uncertainly, rocking a little, gazing intently at the two people before him. They drank him in.

Mr. Pearson knelt on one knee. "Freddie," he said, "come here. Come to Daddy."

Freddie looked back at me for a moment. Then, turning, he walked slowly toward them; and they reached out their arms and gathered him in.

Build Me a Son
General Douglas A. MacArthur

Build me a son, O Lord, who will be strong enough to know when he is weak, and brave enough to face himself when he is afraid; one who will be proud and unbending in honest defeat, and humble and gentle in victory.

Build me a son whose wishbone will not be where his backbone should be; a son who will know Thee—and that to know himself is the foundation stone of knowledge.

Lead him, I pray, not in the path of ease and comfort, but under the stress and spur of difficulties and challenge. Here, let him learn to stand up in the storm; here, let him learn compassion for those who fall.

Build me a son whose heart will be clear, whose goals will be high; a son who will master himself before he seeks to master other men; one who will learn to laugh, yet never forget how to weep; one who will reach into the future, yet never forget the past.

And after all these things are his, add, I pray, enough of a sense of humor, so that he may always be serious, yet never take himself too seriously. Give him humility, so that he may always remember the simplicity of true greatness, the open mind of true wisdom, the meekness of true strength. Then I, his father, will dare to whisper, "I have not lived in vain."

Great Lady

Tim Hansel

I remember when I was in fourth grade and you used to do things like stay up half the night just to make me a Zorro outfit for Halloween. I knew you were a good mom, but I didn't realize what a great lady you were.

I can remember your working two jobs sometimes and running the beauty shop in the front of our home so as to insure that our family would be able to make ends meet. You worked long, long hours and somehow managed to smile all the way through it. I knew you were a hard worker, but I didn't realize what a great lady you were.

I remember the night that I came to you late...in fact, it was near midnight or perhaps beyond, and told you that I was supposed to be a king in a play at school the next day. Somehow you rose to the occasion and created a king's purple robe with ermine on it (made of cotton and black markers). After all that work I still forgot to turn around in the play, so that no one really saw the completion of all your work. Still, you were able to laugh and love and enjoy even those kinds of moments. I knew then that you were a mother like no other who could rise to any occasion, but I didn't realize what a great lady you were.

I remember when I split my head open for the sixth time in a row and you told the school, "He will be okay. Just give him a little rest. I'll come and check on him later." They knew and I knew that you were tough, but I didn't realize what a great lady you were.

I can remember in junior high and high school you helping me muddle through my homework—you making costumes for special events at school—you attending all my games. I knew at the time that you would try almost anything, if it would help one of your children, but I didn't realize what a great lady you were.

I remember bringing forty-three kids home at 3:30 one morning when I worked for Young Life and asking if it would be okay if they stayed over for the night and had breakfast. I remember you getting up at 4:30 to pull off this heroic feat. I knew at the time that you were a joyous and generous giver, but I didn't realize what a great lady you were.

I can remember you attending all my football and basketball games in high school and getting so excited that you hit the person in front of you with your pompons. I could even hear you rooting for me way out in the middle of the field. I knew then that you were one of the classic cheerleaders of all time, but I didn't realize what a great lady you were.

I remember all the sacrifices you made so I could go to Stanford—the extra work you took on, the care packages you sent so regularly, the mail that reminded me that I wasn't in this all alone. I knew you were a great friend, but I didn't realize what a great lady you were.

I remember graduating from Stanford, and deciding to work for two hundred dollars a month loving kids through Young Life. Although you and Dad thought I had fallen off the end of the ladder you still encouraged me. In fact, I remember when you came down to help me fix up my little one-room abode. You added your special, loving touch to what would have been very simple quarters. I realized then—and time and time again—what a creative genius you were, but I didn't realize what a great lady you were.

Time wore on, I grew older and got married, and started a family. You became "NaNa" and cherished your new role, yet you never seemed to grow older. I realized then that God had carved out a special place in life when he made you, but I didn't realize what a great, great lady you were.

I got slowed down by an accident. Things got a little tougher for me. But you stood alongside as you always had.

Some things, I thought, never change—and I was deeply grateful. I realized then what I had known for a long time— what a great nurse you can be—but I didn't realize what a great, great lady you were.

I wrote some books, and people seemed to like them. You and Dad were so proud that sometimes you gave people copies of the books just to show what one of your kids had done. I realized then what a great promoter you were, but I didn't realize what a great, great lady you were.

Times have changed...seasons have passed, and one of the greatest men I have ever known has passed along as well. I can still remember you at the memorial service, standing tall and proud in a brilliant purple dress, reminding people, "How blessed we have been, and how thankful we are for 'a life well lived.'" In those moments I saw a woman who could stand tall and grateful amidst the most difficult of circumstances. I was beginning to discover what a great, great lady you are.

In the last year, when you have had to stand alone as never before, all of what I have observed and experienced all those years have come together in a brand new way. In spite of it all, now your laughter is richer, your strength is stronger, your love is deeper, and I am discovering in truth what a great, great lady you are.

Thanks for choosing me to be one of your sons.

Tim

Life

BEAUTIFUL THINGS
Helen Keller

*The best and the most beautiful things in life
cannot be seen or even touched…
they must be felt with the heart.*

Kennedy's Question

Billy Graham

Just a few days before president-elect John F. Kennedy was to be inaugurated, I was invited to join him and Senator George Smathers in Florida for a golf game and an evening visit at the Kennedy compound in Palm Beach. As we were driving back from the golf course, President Kennedy parked the car, turned to me and asked, "Do you believe Jesus Christ is coming back to earth again?" I was dumbfounded at his question. For one thing, I never dreamed that Mr. Kennedy would ask a question like that, and for another, I wasn't even sure that he knew Jesus was supposed to come back! Having only been with him a few times prior to that incident I had no grasp of his religious knowledge. "Yes, sir, I do," I replied.

"All right," he said. "Explain it to me." So for several minutes I had the opportunity to talk to him about the second coming of Jesus Christ. I have often wondered why he asked that question, and I think part of the answer came a thousand days later when he was assassinated. Cardinal Cushing read the verses I've quoted [below] at President Kennedy's funeral, and millions of people watched and heard the services around the world.

That statement in verse 17 especially stands out: *we who are alive on that day will be caught up together with those who have gone before to meet the Lord in the air.* That phrase, "caught up," is the translation of a Greek word which means to snatch away. The day is fast approaching when Jesus Christ will come back to "snatch away" His followers from all the graveyards of the world, and those of us who are alive and remain will join them in the great escape! That is the hope of the future for the Christian.

For the Lord himself shall descend from heaven with a shout, with the voice of the archangel, and with the trump of

God: *and the dead in Christ will rise first: Then we which are alive and remain shall be caught up together with them in the clouds, to meet the Lord in the air: and so shall we ever be with the Lord. Wherefore comfort one another with these words.*

1 Thessalonians 4:16–17 (KJV)

TRUSTING

Alice Marquardt

*I do not understand it
but I just keep trusting my Good Shepherd
because I know He will not lead me
anyplace He does not want me to follow.*

If We Had Hurried

Billy Rose

There once was a fellow who, with his dad, farmed a little piece of land. Several times a year they would load up the old ox-drawn cart with vegetables and go into the nearest city to sell their produce. Except for their name and the patch of ground, father and son had little in common. The old man believed in taking it easy. The boy was usually in a hurry...the go-getter type.

One morning, bright and early, they hitched up the ox to the loaded cart and started on the long journey. The son figured that if they walked faster, kept going all day and night, they'd make the market by early the next morning. So he kept prodding the ox with a stick, urging the beast to get a move on.

"Take it easy, son," said the old man. "You'll last longer."

"But if we get to the market ahead of the others, we'll have a better chance of getting good prices," argued the son.

No reply. Dad just pulled his hat down over his eyes and fell asleep on the seat. Itchy and irritated, the young man kept goading the ox to walk faster. His stubborn pace refused to change.

Four hours and four miles down the road, they came to a little house. The father woke up, smiled and said, "Here's your uncle's place. Let's stop in and say hello."

"But we've lost an hour already," complained the hotshot.

"Then a few more minutes won't matter. My brother and I live so close, yet we see each other so seldom," the father answered slowly.

The boy fidgeted and fumed while the two old men laughed and talked away almost an hour. On the move again, the man took his turn leading the ox. As they approached a fork in the road, the father led the ox to the right.

"The left is the shorter way," said the son.

"I know it," replied the old man, "but this way is so much prettier."

"Have you no respect for time?" the young man asked impatiently.

"Oh, I respect it very much! That's why I like to look at beauty and enjoy each moment to the fullest."

The winding path led through graceful meadows, wildflowers, and along a rippling stream—all of which the young man missed as he churned within, preoccupied and boiling with anxiety. He didn't even notice how lovely the sunset was that day.

Twilight found them in what looked like a huge, colorful garden. The old man breathed in the aroma, listened to the bubbling brook, and pulled the ox to a halt. "Let's sleep here," he sighed.

"This is the last trip I'm taking with you," snapped his son. "You're more interested in watching sunsets and smelling flowers than in making money!"

"Why, that's the nicest thing you've said in a long time," smiled the dad. A couple of minutes later he was snoring—as his boy glared back at the stars. The night dragged slowly, the son was restless.

Before sunrise the young man hurriedly shook his father awake. They hitched up and went on. About a mile down the road they happened upon another farmer—a total stranger—trying to pull his cart out of a ditch.

"Let's give him a hand," whispered the old man.

"And lose more time?" the boy exploded.

"Relax, son...you might be in a ditch sometime yourself. We need to help others in need—don't forget that." The boy looked away in anger.

It was almost eight o'clock that morning by the time the other cart was back on the road. Suddenly, a great flash split the sky. What sounded like thunder followed. Beyond the hills, the sky grew dark.

"Looks like big rain in the city," said the old man.

"If we had hurried, we'd be almost sold out by now," grumbled his son.

"Take it easy...you'll last longer. And you'll enjoy life so much more," counseled the kind old gentleman.

It was late in the afternoon by the time they got to the hill overlooking the city. They stopped and stared down at it for a long, long time. Neither of them said a word. Finally, the young man put his hand on his father's shoulder and said, "I see what you mean, Dad."

They turned their cart around and began to roll slowly away from what had once been the city of Hiroshima.

Spring Filly

Nancy Spiegelberg

Spirited spring filly
flicking your head
sniffing the warm
newness of the breeze
What a beauty
you are
running free
over the fresh
green earth
Don't you know
to be of use
to your master
you must be broken?

LAUGHTER

Tim Hansel

He who laughs...lasts.

The Hammer, The File, and The Furnace

Charles R. Swindoll

It was the enraptured Rutherford who said in the midst of very painful trials and heartaches:

Praise God for the hammer, the file, and the furnace!

Let's think about that. The hammer is a useful and handy instrument. It is an essential and helpful tool, if nails are ever to be driven into place. Each blow forces them to bite deeper as the hammer's head pounds and pounds.

But if the nail had feelings and intelligence, it would give us another side of the story. To the nail, the hammer is a brutal, relentless master—an enemy who loves to beat it into submission. That is the nail's view of the hammer. It is correct. Except for one thing. The nail tends to forget that both it and the hammer are held by the same workman. The workman decides whose "head" will be pounded out of sight...and which hammer will be used to do the job.

This decision is the sovereign right of the carpenter. Let the nail but remember that it and the hammer are held by the same workman...and its resentment will fade as it yields to the carpenter without complaint.

The same analogy holds true for the metal that endures the rasp of the file and the blast of the furnace. If the metal forgets that it and the tools are objects of the same craftsman's care, it will build up hatred and resentment. The metal must keep in mind that the craftsman knows what he's doing...and is doing what is best.

Heartaches and disappointments are like the hammer, the file, and the furnace. They come in all shapes and sizes: an unfulfilled romance, a lingering illness and untimely death, an unachieved goal in life, a broken home or marriage, a severed friendship, a wayward and rebellious child, a personal medical report that advises "immediate surgery," a failing grade at school, a depression that simply won't go away, a habit you can't seem to break. Sometimes heartaches come suddenly ... other times they appear over the passing of many months, slowly as the erosion of earth.

Do I write to a "nail" that has begun to resent the blows of the hammer? Are you at the brink of despair, thinking that you cannot bear another day of heartache? Is that what's gotten you down?

As difficult as it may be for you to believe this today, the Master knows what He's doing. Your Savior knows your breaking point. The bruising and crushing and melting process is designed to reshape you, not ruin you. Your value is increasing the longer He lingers over you.

Three Men and a Bridge
Sandy Snavely

The bridge has become a kind of good old friend to me. When I first began crossing it every morning on my way to work, it was the signal that my long trip was nearly finished. But after a time I began to focus instead on the people walking across the bridge. The Ross Island Bridge is one of the few bridges in Portland where walkers are as welcome as drivers. There was the young black man who I would pass by almost every morning. His intelligent and handsome face also seemed determined and driven. I started praying for him, for his day and for his life. When we didn't meet on the bridge, I found myself deeply concerned for him. Now he's never there. I wonder where he is, how he is. Was he a student? Did he finish school? Did he become ill while forging through the wicked winter weather? Or did he simply buy a car and join the morning commute on wheels?

Then there is the older man who is occasionally seen with a large metal cross hoisted over one shoulder with a sign on his back that reads, "Jesus saves sinner from hell." My stomach always churns when I see him. He's not as easy to pray for as my young black friend. Maybe it's because I'm not as bold in my faith as he. Maybe it's because though his cross gives the appearance of being large and heavy to carry, it is actually supported by a small cart of wheels. There's just something about that picture that makes me uncomfortable.

But the portrait that has found the deepest place in my memory is that of a homeless man and his dog. The man was unshaved and disheveled. He wore an old camouflaged army jacket, trousers and military boots. He had long hair, not yet turned in color by age. His backpack was heavily packed, pulling his shoulders forward. Although this scene was not unusual for the area, I guess it was the dog that brought such love to the picture. He was a big, old and obviously loyal black Labrador. He carried a backpack also. It had two canvas pouches that were well balanced on each side of his chest. The man and his dog poignantly displayed the heart of true friendship. How many times in my own life have I longed to have my bundles of burdens so affectionately carried.

My young black friend drew me to pray for him, for he was needy in spirit. The old man with the cross harshly illustrated the need for gentleness and authenticity when sharing my faith. But it was the homeless man and his dog who reminded me of the deep longing of every soul, the cry of every heart. To have one at your side whose love is so unconditional and uncompromising, who refuses to cast blame or to judge the hows and whys of the burden, but instead comes alongside and shoulders the load. There's a profound privilege in being both the burdened and burden bearer, to be needy and to be needed.

As I continue my journeys through life, I know there will be many bridges yet to cross. Whether forging ahead or just struggling with a friend to get to the other side, I will treasure in my heart the lessons from three men and the bridge.

Incredible!

David Jeremiah

It happened around noon on Mother's Day. According to a national news report, twenty-seven-year-old Michael Murray decided to take his two children to the medical center in Massachusetts where their mother was on duty as a surgical nurse. The family wanted to drop off some Mother's Day presents: a gold necklace with the words "number 1 Mom," and a single rose. With their mission accomplished, the father and his two children made their way back to the darkened indoor garage where the car had been parked.

Murray gently set the infant seat and three-month-old Matthew on the sun roof of the car and turned his attention to buckling Matthew's twenty-month-old sister into her seat. Without thinking further, Murray slid into the driver's seat and drove off, forgetting that Matthew was still on the roof.

Moving slowly from the darkened garage into the bright sunlight, Murray drove through busy streets toward Interstate 290. Despite heavy traffic, nobody beeped or waved to warn him that anything was wrong. Pulling onto the expressway that cuts through the city, the driver accelerated to 50 mph and then he heard it, a scraping on the roof of his car as the tiny seat with Matthew strapped in began to slide. He said, "I looked to where Matthew should have been in the car, and then in the rear view mirror I saw him sliding down the highway in his infant seat. "That's where he landed. In the middle of the interstate, in the path of oncoming traffic...."

*****

The car seat flew off the roof and hit the road and was sliding down the highway almost as fast as the cars were coming toward it. An antique dealer named James Boothby was following the Murray car when he saw the whole event unfold. He saw young Matthew sail off the roof and hit the road.

He said:

I saw something in the air. At first I thought someone had thrown some garbage out the window. Then I saw it and thought it was a doll. Then the doll opened its mouth and I realized this was a little baby. It just landed on the road. It bounced a couple of times, and it never tipped over. It just landed on the road and slid along a bit. I slammed on my car brakes and turned my car around in the lane so that no other cars could go by. I jumped from the car, and I ran and found an uninjured baby in an undamaged car seat, and scooped him up in my arms and took him back and gave him to his petrified father.

That true story has to be as close to a grade A miracle as anything you and I have ever experienced. God intervened in that situation or it would have been an incredible tragedy.

Struggles

Retold by Alice Gray

When he was a small boy, he had loved butterflies. Oh, not to net and mount them, but to wonder at their designs and habits.

Now a grown man with his first son to be born in a few weeks, he found himself once again fascinated with a cocoon. He had found it at the side of the park path. Somehow the twig had been knocked from the tree and the cocoon had survived undamaged and still woven to the branch.

As he had seen his mother do, he gently protected it by wrapping it in his handkerchief and carried it home. The cocoon found a temporary home in a wide-top mason jar with holes in the lid. The jar was placed on the mantle for easy viewing and protection from their curious cat who would delight in volleying the sticky silk between her paws.

The man watched. His wife's interest lasted only a moment, but he studied the silky envelope. Almost imperceptibly at first, the cocoon moved. He watched more closely and soon the cocoon was trembling with activity. Nothing else happened. The cocoon remained tightly glued to the twig and there was no sign of wings.

Finally the shaking became so intense, the man thought the butterfly would die from the struggle. He removed the lid on the jar, took a sharp pen knife from his desk drawer, and carefully made a tiny slit in the side of the cocoon. Almost immediately, one wing appeared and then outstretched the other. The butterfly was free!

It seemed to enjoy its freedom and walked along the edge of the mason jar and along the edge of the mantle. But it didn't fly. At first the man thought the wings needed time to dry, but time passed and still the butterfly did not take off.

The man was worried and called up his neighbor who

taught high school science. He told the neighbor how he had found the cocoon, placed it in the mason jar, and the terrible trembling as the butterfly struggled to get out. When he described how he had carefully made a small slit in the cocoon, the teacher stopped him. "Oh, that is the reason. You see, the struggle is what gives the butterfly the strength to fly."

And so it is with us. Sometimes it's the struggles in life that strengthen our faith the most.

He Listened

Joseph Bayly
Written after he laid three of his sons in the grave.

I was sitting, torn by grief. Someone came and talked to me of God's dealings, of why it happened, of hope beyond the grave. He talked constantly, he said things I knew were true. I was unmoved except to wish he'd go away. He finally did.

Another came and sat beside me. He just sat beside me for an hour and more, listened when I said something, answered briefly, prayed simply, left. I was moved. I was comforted. I hated to see him go.

I BELIEVE

Written on a wall in a concentration camp

I believe in the sun
even when it is not shining
I believe in love
even when I feel it not
I believe in God
even when He is silent.

Do You Wish to Get Well?

Kay Arthur

D o you wish to get well?" It seems like a rather foolish question on the surface! At first you think, "Who wouldn't wish to get well?"

I ask these questions, and my mind races to a man sitting at one of the gates surrounding the Old City of Jerusalem. As I recently came out of the Old City into the noise of the lumbering buses jammed to the doors with Arabs and to the honking of irate, impassioned cab drivers, as I felt the bright sunshine which had been shielded by the walled, crowded, narrow streets of the Old City, a man sitting on the ground caught my attention. He was happily conversing with other beggars until a foreign tourist came by. At that point, all conversation ceased, and a hand was lifted as dark eyes silently pled for alms. The other hand pulled up a pant leg to make sure the already exposed ulcer—bright pink, glazed over with white purulent patches glistening in the sun—was not missed.

My nurse's heart brought my feet to a halt. I wanted to bend down and shield the open wound from the dust sent flying by the traffic scurrying through the gate. His leg needed tending. It should be washed, medicated, and dressed by someone who cared. Why, unattended, it would only eat away until it reached his bone, and then he could lose his leg!

Arrested by his plight, I stopped to gaze at his leg and look into the darkness of his eyes, until my friend gently took me by my elbow and propelled me toward our destination. I was a tourist and did not know about these things. She then proceeded to tell me that this man did not wish to be made well. He made his living from his wound. No need to confront the complexities of responsibility as a citizen of Israel when one could merely sit down in the dust and dirt of Jerusalem and receive pity along with a few shekels.

My wounded beggar could have been healed. The hospital doors were open to him and medicine was available, but he did not wish to get well. As I looked back in curious fascination, I caught one last glimpse of someone less than what he could have been.

The man in John 5 had been sick for 38 years. We do not know how long he had been lying beside the pool of Bethesda. All we know is that when Jesus passed by and asked him if he wished to be made well, he had to make a choice. Either he could continue in his normal habit of life, or he could relinquish it for healing.

Suppose, Beloved, Jesus asked you if you wanted to be made well—emotionally, physically, spiritually? What would you answer?

Heritage

Sally J. Knower

T he old rocker cracked and popped as Jenny set it in motion with a push of her hand. The springs poked their wire heads above the faded horsehair covering. Even in the dimly lit attic she could see the wood was scarred and the varnish worn away. She tugged the relic to the stairwell and slid it, one step at a time, carefully balancing the awkward weight against her watermelon belly. At the bottom of the stairs she kneaded the muscles at her lower back.

"Jenny Lester, what did you do? You shouldn't have brought the chair down by yourself," Audrea Lester scolded.

"I'm all right, Mother Lester."

The baby squirmed and kicked its objections. She laughingly rubbed the rebel pushing from within. "You just wait. Someday I'll rock you in Grandmother Lester's chair."

Clara and Harry Lester bought the chair shortly after their wedding in 1889. They moved it by horse and wagon from the secondhand store in Lincoln, Nebraska, to their farm outside of Fairbury. Harry refinished the wood. Clara upholstered its back and seat with fashionable horsehair material. Only special, come-into-the-parlor company like Reverend Jorganson used it until the babies came. Then Clara niched it between the wood stove and table in the all-purpose kitchen.

As she soothed babies with its cadence the chair became hers. She'd touch down between stirring the stew and slopping the sows they raised. Tea towel harnesses secured toddlers to the chair while she canned and preserved.

She anxiously shuttled the chair to and fro when scarlet fever made her third born delirious. "God, if you're really out there," she railed, "help my little one." When healing came, tears of relief sprinkled her apron. "God, I believe you are real. You heard me. Thank you for saving my son. He is yours now,

Lord, and so am I."

The chair became her altar and her podium. She tucked her feet up on it and leaned toward the lamp to read her Bible, then faced it into the corner to form a prayer closet.

The chair kept rhythm with the songs she sang from quiet lullabies to joyous hallelujahs. It fairly jumped with her tapping toe when Harry squeezed music from his concertina.

Clara darned socks for her growing sons and snapped beans while seated on its broad cushion. When grandchildren came they teethed on the chair's arms.

She sat in the chair and captivated progeny with true stories of adventure like the day the rabid dog ran through the farmyard without biting anyone, or when the tornado blew the shingles from the roof and no one was hurt. She told about Shadrach, Meshach and Abednego surviving the fiery furnace and how David slew Goliath.

The chair sat by the four-poster bed as Harry wrestled with cancer. Clara sat vigilant at his side and held his hand. After he died she pulled the chair close to the stove and wondered if she would ever feel warm again.

Taxes grew but funds didn't. Clara's resources diminished. The farm had to be sold. She rocked and watched as piece by piece, equipment and furnishings were auctioned. It was like tearing strips from her life to see them go. Clara kept only the chair. She took it with her when she went to live with her youngest son, Robert, and his wife, Audrea.

Audrea made room for the chair. It looked incongruous beside French Provincial in the town house. She made Clara welcome but Clara felt as comfortable as a corn in a Sunday shoe.

Then Jimmy was born. The last little grandson to rock in her arms and tug at her hair. As he grew she shrank. Low oxygen days fogged her mind. Only her God and her chair remained familiar. Alien noises—fire engines, horns and

squealing brakes—interrupted her sleep. Clara endured restless hours wrapped in a quilt rocking and praying and waiting
to go home.

After her death the worn old chair was relegated to
Jimmy's room. He was delighted to have it. He used it to hunt
tigers. He drove horses from the chariot it formed. He did
homework in it as he kept time to his raucous radio. He
dreamed dreams and planned his future within its circle.

The chair developed a popping sound under the weight of
a boy turned man.

When he went away to college his old room became a
guest room and den. The rocker disappeared.

A freckled coed caught Jimmy's fancy and he courted her
his senior year. They married. Jenny worked while he went to
seminary. He got the call to his first church hand-in-hand
with the call to fatherhood.

Their first child grew and stretched beneath Jenny's heart.
"I wish we had my grandmother's chair," Jimmy said as he
lightly touched Jenny's bulging front. "You could rock our son
in it."

"Or daughter," Jenny countered.

"That old rocker was special. I felt so proud when the chair
was given to me. I wonder where it is now."

"Mother Lester," Jenny asked the next time she saw her
mother-in-law, "What ever became of the rocking chair
Jimmy used to have in his room?"

"It's in the attic," Audrea answered.

"I'd like to see it. I have an idea."

"Come on, I'll show it to you. It's in bad shape. You can see
the stuffing is coming out and the wood is marred." Audrea
said as she switched on the attic light.

Jenny rubbed her hand across the back of the rocker. "The
scars aren't deep. They just add character. It will take work
but I think it can be fixed. Can I try? I'd like to surprise

Jimmy. It would be a terrific anniversary gift."

"You can if you want to. In fact, you can work on it in Jimmy's old room."

As Mother Lester readied the spare room Jenny brought the chair down from the attic. She was so anxious to begin.

Beautiful oak came out of hiding as Jenny stripped the old surface and sanded it smooth. The wood glowed softly under new varnish. Jenny tied down the old springs. They were snug and comfortable under the new coverings. It looked very handsome with clean claw feet and trimly tucked back.

On celebration day Jenny draped a ribbon, Miss America style, across the chair's shoulders.

"What are you up to, Jenny Lester?" her husband asked as she led him up the stairs to his old room. "Your grin gives you away."

"Close your eyes while I open the door. Better put your hands over them too." He dutifully covered up. "Now, no peeking."

"You act like an excited little kid," Jimmy chuckled. "Are you sure you're old enough to have my son?"

"Okay," she said after positioning him in front of the rocker. "You can look. Happy anniversary."

"Grandmother Lester's rocker! Oh, honey, its wonderful," he exclaimed as he draped Jenny's torso with the Miss America ribbon.

That evening at home, next to the full-sized bed, Jimmy rocked Jenny on his lap.

"You'd better let me up," Jenny said as the chair cracked and popped. "It's complaining."

"No you don't," Jimmy said as Jenny tried to rise. "You aren't going anywhere. It's not complaining. It's just talking to us."

"So it has a voice of its own does it? It almost has a life of its own," Jenny mused.

"It certainly has a heritage," Jimmy said. "When our son is born I am going to tell him about the heritage of faith that began with Grandmother Lester and came down four generations to him."

"Or her," Jenny countered sleepily.

Old Age—It's Later Than You Think

Anonymous

It's later than you think—everything is farther away now than it used to be. It's twice as far to the corner—and they added a hill. I notice I've given up running for the bus—it leaves faster than it used to. It seems to me they are making steps steeper than in the old days and have you noticed the smaller print they use in the newspapers? There is no sense asking anyone to read aloud...everyone speaks in such a low voice I can scarcely hear them. Material in dresses is so skimpy especially around the hips. It's all but impossible to reach my shoe laces. Even people are changing—they are much younger than they used to be when I was their age. On the other hand, people my age are much older than I. I ran into an old classmate the other day and she had aged so much she didn't remember me. I got to thinking about the poor thing while I was combing my hair this morning and I glanced in the mirror at my reflection and confound it, they don't make mirrors like they used to either....

The Orchestra

Judy Urschel Straalsund

There was once a town with an orchestra. The Orchestra had every kind of instrument you could possibly imagine. From banjos to bagpipes, piccolos to pianos, castanets to cornets.

It was an honor and a privilege to be a member of The Orchestra though there were no musical requirements to get in. The Conductor had offered a standing invitation to anyone who would like to join, with one stipulation. The contract was for life. Some instrumentalists refused to join because they were afraid that such an agreement would stifle their artistic creativity. Others worried about what would happen if they didn't like the music the Conductor would give them to play.

The Conductor had given all His musicians the score of a piece He had composed called "The Grand Finale," and He asked them to practice it in preparation for the coming of the Concert Day. Each section took its part seriously and practiced very diligently. But the musicians couldn't help noticing that some of the other sections were practicing differently than they were.

"Look at those violins," groused the French horn section. "There's no rhyme nor reason to the way they practice—it's something different every time. Why don't they do what we do and practice the scales and etudes? They have no understanding of the fundamentals!"

"I declare," sniffed the violinists as they observed a French horn rehearsal. "It's hard to believe they always do the exact same thing. It must be so boring! Why don't they do what we do and let the joy of the music take them wherever it will?"

"Can you believe it?" gasped the drummers. "All those bassoonists ever do is go to their stuffy practice room and back home again. They don't have any experience playing for other people at all; they've got to be getting stagnant."

"Sometimes it makes you wonder if they really signed the contract," sighed the bassoonists. "Those drummers are so busy; out on the town every night, playing in the worst kinds of places. They probably don't spend any time practicing at all."

Once some of the musicians chanced to meet, and of course their conversation centered on the way to interpret the score.

"It's a victory march," the trumpet player announced decisively. "It is meant to be played with a solemn yet triumphal air."

"No, no," the harpist declared. "It's a love song—sweet and joyous and tender."

"That's crazy!" the clarinet player interrupted. "It's a hymn —reverent and worshipful."

Though there were many sectional rehearsals, the players could never agree on when to rehearse as a full orchestra, so no one knew how the piece would finally sound. And they disagreed so violently about the time and conditions of the performance, it was better not to bring up the subject at all.

The town still has its orchestra. The sections are still rehearsing. But those who hear them, wonder. Will they really be ready to play together when the Conductor raises His baton on the Concert Day?

Do You Know Who His Daddy Is?

Zig Ziglar

In his beautiful book *Rising Above the Crowd*, Brian Harbour tells the story of Ben Hooper. When Ben Hooper was born many years ago in the foothills of East Tennessee, little boys and girls like Ben who were born to unwed mothers were ostracized and treated terribly. By the time he was three years old, the other children would scarcely play with him. Parents were saying idiotic things like, "What's a boy like that doing playing with our children?" as if the child had anything at all to do with his own birth.

Saturday was the toughest day of all. Ben's mom would take him down to the little general store to buy their supplies for the week. Invariably, the other parents in the store would make caustic remarks just loudly enough for both mother and child to hear, comments like, "Did you ever figure out who his daddy is?" What a tough, tough childhood.

In those days there was no kindergarten. So, at age six, little Ben entered the first grade. He was given his own desk, as were all the children. At recess, he stayed at that little desk and studied because none of the other children would play with him. At noon, little Ben could be found eating his sack lunch all alone. The happy chatter of the children who shunned him was barely audible from where he sat.

It was a big event when anything changed in the foothills of East Tennessee, and when little Ben was twelve years old a new preacher came to pastor the little church in Ben's town.

Almost immediately, little Ben started hearing exciting things about him—about how loving and nonjudgmental he was. How he accepted people just as they were, and when he was with them, he made them feel like the most important people in the world. Reportedly, the preacher had charisma. When he walked into a group of any size, anywhere, the entire complexion of that group changed. Their smiles broadened, their laughter increased, and their spirits rose.

One Sunday, though he had never been to church a day in his life, little Ben Hooper decided he was going to go and hear the preacher. He got there late and he left early because he did not want to attract any attention, but he liked what he heard. For the first time in that young boy's life, he caught just a glimmer of hope.

Ben was back in church the next Sunday and the next and the next. He always got there late and always left early, but his hope was building each Sunday.

On about the sixth or seventh Sunday the message was so moving and exciting that Ben became absolutely enthralled with it. It was almost as if there were a sign behind the preacher's head that read, "For you, little Ben Hooper of unknown parentage, there is hope!" Ben got so wrapped up in the message, he forgot about the time and didn't notice that a number of people had come in after he had taken his seat.

Suddenly, the services were over. Ben very quickly stood up to leave as he had in all the Sundays past, but the aisles were clogged with people and he could not run out. As he was working his way through the crowd, he felt a hand on his shoulder. He turned around and looked up, right into the eyes of the young preacher who asked him a question that had been on the mind of every person there for the last twelve years: "Whose boy are you?"

Instantly, the church grew deathly quiet. Slowly, a smile started to spread across the face of the young preacher until it broke into a huge grin, and he exclaimed, "Oh! I know whose boy you are! Why, the family resemblance is unmistakable. You are a child of God!"

And with that the young preacher swatted him across the

rear and said, "That's quite a heritage you've got there, boy! Now, go and see to it that you live up to it."

LEADERSHIP

Author unknown

Are you a leader?
Look behind and see if anyone is following.
He who thinks he is leading
and no one is following
is only taking a walk.

Let Go

Dr. Billy Graham

A little child playing one day with a very valuable vase put his hand into it and could not withdraw it. His father, too, tried his best, but all in vain. They were thinking of breaking the vase when the father said, "Now, my son, make one more try. Open your hand and hold your fingers out straight as you see me doing, and then pull."

To their astonishment the little fellow said, "O no, father. I couldn't put my fingers out like that, because if I did I would drop my penny."

Smile, if you will—but thousands of us are like that little boy, so busy holding on to the world's worthless penny that we cannot accept liberation. I beg you to drop that trifle in your heart. Surrender! Let go, and let God have His way in your life.

The Runaways

Cliff Schimmels

One winter morning the year before I started to school, my dad came in and asked if I would like to go with him to feed the cows. That sounded like fun, so I dressed in my warmest clothes, including the mittens connected by a string through the sleeves of my jacket, and went out with my dad to take my place in the world of work.

It was a pleasant morning. The sun was shining brightly, but it was cold and the ground was covered with a blanket of new snow. We harnessed the team, Babe and Blue, and went over the hill with a wagon full of hay. After we had found the cows and unloaded the hay for them, we started home. Then my dad came up with a good idea. "Would you like to drive?" he asked. And I responded in typical manly fashion. I like to drive anything: cars, trucks, golf carts or donkey carts. I think the attraction must be the power. There is such a sense of power to be in control of something larger than I am, and it's good for my male ego.

I took the lines from my dad, held them looped over my hands as he showed me, and we plodded back home. I was thrilled. I was in control. I was driving. But the plodding bothered me. I decided that while I was in control, we should speed up, so I clucked the horses along and they began to hurry. First they began to trot, and I decided that was a much better pace. We were moving along and we would get home much faster. But Babe and Blue came up with a better idea. They decided that if they would run, we would get home even sooner.

The horses went to work on their plan and began to run. As I remember it, they were running as fast as I have ever seen horses run, but that observation might have a slight exaggeration factor built in. But they did run. The wagon bounced from mound to mound. As the prairie dog holes whizzed by, I concluded that we were in a dangerous situation, and I started to try my best to slow down this runaway team. I pulled and tugged on the lines until my hands cramped. I cried and pleaded, but nothing worked. Old Babe and Blue just kept running.

I glanced over at my dad, and he was just sitting there, looking out across the pasture and watching the world go by. By now, I was frantic. My hands were cut from the lines, the tears streaming down my face were almost frozen from the winter cold, and stuff was running out my nose. And my dad was just sitting there watching the world go by.

Finally, in utter desperation, I turned to him and said as calmly as I could, "Here, Daddy, I don't want to drive anymore."

Now that I am older and people call me Grandpa, I reenact that scene at least once a day. Regardless of who we are, how old we are, how wise or how powerful we are, there is always that moment when our only response is to turn to our Father and say, "Here, I don't want to drive anymore."

Broken Dreams

Author unknown

As children bring their broken toys
    with tears for us to mend
    I brought my broken dreams to God
because He is my friend.
But then, instead of leaving Him
in peace to work alone
I hung around and tried to help
with ways that were my own.
At last I snatched them back and cried,
"How can you be so slow?"
"My child," He said, "What could I do...
you never did let go."

CHANGE

Martin Luther King, Jr.

I believe that what self-centered men have torn down,
other-centered men can build up.

Significance

Joni Eareckson Tada

Every morning Connie opens Diane's door to begin the long routine of exercising and bathing her severely paralyzed friend.

The sun's rays slant through the blinds, washing the room in a soft, golden glow. The folds of the covers haven't moved since Connie pulled them up around Diane the night before. Yet she can tell her friend has been awake for awhile.

"Are you ready to get up yet?"

"No...not yet," comes the weak reply from under the covers.

Connie sighs, smiles, and clicks shut the door.

The story is the same each dawn of every new day at Connie and Diane's apartment. The routine rarely changes. Sunrise stretches into mid-morning by the time Diane is ready to sit up in her wheel chair. But those long hours in bed are significant.

In her quiet sanctuary, Diane turns her head slightly on the pillow toward the corkboard on the wall. Her eyes scan each thumb-tacked card and list. Each photo. Every torn piece of paper carefully pinned in a row. The stillness is broken as Diane begins to murmur.

She is praying.

Some would look at Diane—stiff and motionless—and shake their heads. She has to be fed everything, pushed everywhere. The creeping limitations of multiple sclerosis encroach further each year. Her fingers are curled and rigid. Her voice is barely a whisper. People might look at her and say, "What a shame. Her life has no meaning. She can't really do anything."

But Diane is confident, convinced her life is significant. Her labor of prayer counts.

She moves mountains that block the paths of missionaries.

She helps open the eyes of the spiritually blind in southeast Asia.

She pushes back the kingdom of darkness that blackens the alleys and streets of the gangs in east LA.

She aids the homeless mothers...single parents...abused children...despondent teenagers...handicapped boys...and dying and forgotten old people in the nursing home down the street where she lives.

Diane is on the front lines, advancing the Gospel of Christ, holding up weak saints, inspiring doubting believers, energizing other prayer warriors, and delighting her Lord and Savior.

This meek and quiet woman sees her place in the world; it doesn't matter that others may not recognize her significance in the grand scheme of things. In fact, she's not unlike Emily in *Our Town* who signs her address as:

> Grovers Corner
> New Hampshire
> United States of America
> Western Hemisphere
> Planet Earth
> Solar System
> The Universe
> Mind of God

In the mind of God...that's about as significant as you can get, whether you sit at a typewriter, behind the wheel of a bus, at the desk in a classroom, in a chair by your kitchen table...or lay in bed and pray. Your life is hidden with Christ. You enrich His inheritance. You are His ambassador. In Him your life has depth and meaning and purpose, no matter what you do.

Someone has said, "The point of this life...is to become the person God can love perfectly, to satisfy His thirst to love. Being counts more than doing, the singer more than the song. We had better stop looking for escape hatches, for this is our hatchery."

It's my prayer that...you will discover the significance that has been yours all along as a child of the King. You may not be able to know the full meaning of every event, but you can know that every event is meaningful.

And you are significant.

DARK ENOUGH
Ralph Waldo Emerson

When it is dark enough, men see stars.

Somebody Loved Him
Rebecca Manley Pippert

He was an eastern European Jew. He had prospered professionally, married a Gentile and had one son. Then came World War II and the deportation of the Jews. His Jewish identity was not widely known, and because of his marriage he thought he might be protected from going to prison camp. But one day as he returned home from work, he saw to his horror that the Gestapo were waiting for him. They grabbed him and led him off to the train. His mind was dazed, wondering who had betrayed him. As they were dragging him away, he cried out to one of the soldiers that he hadn't even been allowed to embrace his wife before he left.

The soldier laughed grimly and said, "You fool. Don't you know that it was your wife who tipped us off?"

"You liar!" Jacob cried. "She would never do a thing like that!"

But the soldier replied, "Then you must be the only one who doesn't know. Your wife is having an affair with the chief of police." Jacob looked back at his wife in disbelief and horror. But the expression of guilt on her face and her inability to look him in the eyes confirmed that it was true.

He spent the next five years in a prison camp. Several times he nearly died. He certainly hoped that he would. The bitterness and despair that filled him was the only reminder that he was still alive. One thing, however, occasionally gave him a flicker of hope. If he could survive prison camp, perhaps his son would still be home and they could be reunited. That was the only thought that ever brought light into his darkness.

Finally the war was over and he was released. As he made the long journey home only one thought obsessed him: the intense desire to see his son. When he arrived at his hometown he was told that his wife had left years before to an unknown destination. Somewhere in northern Europe, he was told. She had taken their son with her. He now knew that he would never see his son again. His last hope was gone. He was physically ill, emaciated, desperately hungry, and penniless. He had nowhere to go, so he went to a park bench where the bums of the town gathered.

Even in his misery he could not overlook the irony. These were the men that he had given loose change to on his way to work in days gone by. Now he was one of them. Before long the police arrested him for loitering. He told the police it was a relief. At least in jail he would get some food and a place to sleep. They saw immediately that he was not a skid row bum but a man in desperate straits. They asked him if he had family. He said he had one brother he had not seen since he was a teenager, who now lived in Tel Aviv. The government decided to pay for the ticket to send him there, as they did not know what else to do with him.

Jacob arrived in Israel with no money. He had hardly eaten in a week and was terribly ill. He went to his brother's home and the brother would not let him in the door. That is almost unheard of in Jewish culture, but the brother had not seen him in years and refused to believe that this haggard, decrepit-looking bum at his door was really his brother Jacob. He told him to come back with papers to prove that it was really he. Jacob did not give him the chance to find out. He could not suffer the indignity of one more rejection.

Now he was almost too poor to secure the means to kill himself. And too tired. So he found another park bench where the lowest of the low gathered and he waited to die. He did not eat, because there was nothing to eat. He had actually sunk to begging for food in his own country, but here he could not bear the humiliation of it. All he thought of was death. He knew it would only be days now.

Several days had passed as he lay on the park bench, when

at a distance he saw a blond, freshly scrubbed teenage girl, obviously an American, entering the park with a friend. He wondered what on earth someone so innocent and angelic-looking was doing in a park for derelicts. He closed his eyes. Suddenly he heard a soft voice speaking to him. Jacob opened his eyes and to his astonishment he saw her looking at him with a compassion and sincerity that caught him off guard. It was the first time he had heard anyone speak to him with kindness in six years. He did not know whether he wanted to cry in gratitude or laugh in cynicism. But her concern moved him in spite of himself. "What do you want?" he growled at her.

"Sir, I wasn't even supposed to be here in this park. I got off the bus at the wrong place. But when I saw you, and the terrible sadness in your face I just couldn't leave without telling you something," she said softly.

"Why don't you get back on your bus and leave me alone!" he snapped, appalled as he heard himself sounding as surly as the street people he used to give money to.

"Sir, I was afraid to come over here, but I feel like God is nudging me to tell you something, before I get back on my bus. I wish I knew how to say it better but, well, sir, Jesus loves you. He loves you. He really does."

He looked at her in disbelief. This child was telling him that somebody in heaven loved him? After all the hell he had been through, all the indignity he had suffered, all the rage that had filled his soul for so many years. And now this naive American, who had probably never known a day of real suffering, who had lived a sheltered and protected life, in her innocence, was telling him that some Gentile God loved him. He could not decide whether he was outraged by the audacity, or moved that she took the effort to talk with him. But as he looked up at her face he saw tears streaming down her cheeks, and to his astonishment he began to weep as well.

"No one could love me, child. It's too late for me," he said between sobs.

"No," she replied urgently as she took his thin, gnarled hand into hers. "It's not too late. God will gladly take you if only you'd let him. Just tell him that you want to. He will love you and help you."

He said it was at that moment that he knew that Someone was reaching out to him through her. He could not have imagined a more unlikely messenger. But he knew deep within that he was being offered help in his last hour. But the choice was his. He decided to take it. He prayed with this girl on some park bench in the outskirts of nowhere, in his own language. Then he looked at her and said, "I am thankful to you, more than you can ever know. But I am very sick. I am dying." With that, the girl and the friend who was with her helped him up and they took him by bus to the home where they were staying.

The family nursed Jacob back to health for one entire year. During the course of that year they shared their faith, read to him from the Bible and prayed with him. Eventually what began as a dying man's desperate invitation to God to take his life, became a total commitment of his life and soul to his Messiah. He laughed and said to us, "The problem with you Gentiles is that you always keep forgetting that Jesus is Jewish! He belonged to us first!"

Jacob eventually found a good job, lived in his own apartment and went back to his brother and was reconciled. He came to faith in his mid-fifties; when I met him he was in his early seventies. As long as I live I will never forget the expression on his face as he spoke of what Jesus meant to him. "It would have been so easy," he said, "to have rejected that girl. To have chosen to harbor all the years of resentments and disillusionment in my heart. But to think that God reached out to me, gave me a home and a family who loved me, restored my health, and above all else, filled my heart with a gladness and joy I never knew was possible! You know what I want to do when I get to heaven? I want to be the one who offers a cup of water to everyone else. What could I ever do to express my gratitude to God for all that he has done for me? How will I ever be able to thank Jesus enough? So much has happened in my life since that moment twenty years ago. But the one fact that staggers me most of all, is that the girl was right. Jesus loves me. He really does."

TO ENDURE
William Barclay

*Endurance is not just the ability to bear a hard thing,
but to turn it into glory.*

Homecoming

Michael Broome
Retold by Alice Gray

A missionary doctor had spent forty years of his life ministering in the primitive villages of Africa. Finally, he decided to retire. He wired ahead that he would be returning by ship and gave the date and time of his arrival.

As he was crossing the Atlantic, he thought back over all the years he had spent helping to heal the people of Africa, both physically and spiritually. Then his thoughts raced ahead to the grand homecoming he knew awaited him in America because he had not been home in all forty years.

As the ship pulled into port, the old man's heart swelled with pride as he saw the homecoming that had been prepared. A great crowd of people had gathered, and there was a huge banner saying, "Welcome Home." As the man stepped off the ship onto the dock and awaited a great ovation, his heart sank. Suddenly he realized the people had not gathered to pay tribute to him but to a movie star who had been aboard the same ship.

He waited in anguish with his heart breaking. No one had come to welcome him home. As the crowd disbursed, the old man was left waiting alone. Tilting his face heavenward, he spoke these words, "Oh God, after giving all those years of my life to my fellow man, was it too much to ask that one person—just one person—be here to welcome me home?"

In the quietness of his heart, he seemed to hear the voice of God whisper to him. "You're not home yet. When you come home to me, you *will* be welcomed."

And everyone who has left houses or brothers or sisters
or father or mother or children or fields for my sake will
receive a hundred times as much and will inherit eternal
life.

Matthew 19:29 (NIV)

Picture of Peace
Catherine Marshall

There once was a king who offered a prize to the artist who would paint the best picture of peace. Many artists tried. The king looked at all the pictures. But there were only two he really liked, and he had to choose between them.

One picture was of a calm lake. The lake was a perfect mirror for peaceful towering mountains all around it. Overhead was a blue sky with fluffy white clouds. All who saw this picture thought that it was a perfect picture of peace.

The other picture had mountains, too. But these were rugged and bare. Above was an angry sky, from which rain fell and in which lightning played. Down the side of the mountain tumbled a foaming waterfall. This did not look peaceful at all.

But when the king looked closely, he saw behind the waterfall a tiny bush growing in a crack in the rock. In the bush a mother bird had built her nest. There, in the midst of the rush of angry water, sat the mother bird on her nest—in perfect peace.

Which picture do you think won the prize? The king chose the second picture. Do you know why?

"Because," explained the king, "peace does not mean to be in a place where there is no noise, trouble, or hard work. Peace means to be in the midst of all those things and still be calm in your heart. That is the real meaning of peace."

I Asked...

Anonymous

I asked God for strength,
that I might achieve.
I was made weak, that I might learn to humbly obey....

I asked for health,
that I might do greater things.
I was given infirmity,
that I might do better things....

I asked for riches,
that I might be happy.
I was given poverty,
that I might be wise....

I asked for power,
that I might have the praise of men.
I was given weakness,
that I might feel the need of God....

I asked for all things,
that I might enjoy life.
I was given life,
that I might enjoy all things....

I got nothing I asked for—
but everything that I had hoped for.
Almost despite myself, my unspoken
prayers were answered.

I am, among all,
most richly blessed!

Life Is Like That

Josh McDowell

*If you always do
What you've always done
You'll always be
What you've always been.*

TAPS

Author unknown

Day is done, gone the sun
From the lake, from the hills, from the sky.
Safely rest, all is well! God is nigh.

Faith

*Now faith is being sure of what we hope for
and certain of what we do not see.*

Hebrews 11:1 (NIV)

Where Do You Run?

Kay Arthur

My friend tells the story of something that happened while his dad was deer hunting in the wilds of Oregon.

Cradling his rifle in the crook of his arm, his dad was following an old logging road nearly overgrown by the encroaching forest. It was early evening, and he was just thinking about returning to camp when a noise exploded in the brush nearby. Before he even had a chance to lift his rifle, a small blur of brown and white came shooting up the road straight for him.

My friend laughs as he tells the story.

"It all happened so fast, Dad hardly had time to think. He looked down and there was a little brown cottontail—utterly spent—crowded up against his legs between his boots. The little thing was trembling all over, but it just sat there and didn't budge.

"Now this was really strange. Wild rabbits are frightened of people, and it's not that often you'd ever actually see one—let alone have one come and sit at your feet.

"While Dad was puzzling over this, another player entered the scene. Down the road—maybe twenty yards away—a weasel burst out of the brush. When it saw my dad—and its intended prey sitting at his feet—the predator froze in its tracks, its mouth panting, its eyes glowing red.

"It was then that Dad understood he had stepped into a little life-and-death drama of the forest. The cottontail, exhausted by the chase, was only moments from death. Dad was its last hope of refuge. Forgetting its natural fear and caution, the little animal instinctively crowded up against him for protection from the sharp teeth of its relentless enemy."

My friend's father did not disappoint. He raised his powerful rifle and deliberately shot into the ground just underneath the weasel. The animal seemed to leap almost straight into the air a couple of feet and then rocketed back into the forest as fast as its legs could move.

For a while, the little rabbit didn't stir. It just sat there, huddled at the man's feet in the gathering twilight while he spoke gently to it.

"Where did it go, little one? I don't think he'll be bothering you for a while. Looks like you're off the hook tonight."

Soon the rabbit hopped away from its protector into the forest.

Where, Beloved, do you run in time of need?

Where do you run when the predators of trouble, worry, and fear pursue you?

Where do you hide when your past pursues you like a relentless wolf, seeking your destruction?

Where do you seek protection when the weasels of temptation, corruption, and evil threaten to overtake you?

Where do you turn when your energy is spent...when weakness saps you and you feel you cannot run away any longer?

Do you turn to your protector, the One who stands with arms open wide, waiting for you to come and huddle in the security of all He is?

Dear Bristol

James Dobson

My heart aches for [all] mothers and fathers who have lost a precious child. Indeed, I hear regularly from parents who have experienced a similar tragedy. One family, in particular, stands out in my mind. I learned of their sorrow from the father who sent me a tribute to the memory of his little girl, Bristol. This is what he wrote:

My Dear Bristol,

Before you were born, I prayed for you. In my heart I knew that you would be a little angel. And so you were.

When you were born on my birthday, April 7, it was evident that you were a special gift from the Lord. But how profound a gift you turned out to be! More than the beautiful bundle of gurgles and rosy cheeks—more than the first-born of my flesh, a joy unspeakable—you showed me God's love more than anything else in all creation. Bristol, you taught me how to love.

I certainly loved you when you were cuddly and cute, when you rolled over and sat up and jabbered your first words. I loved you when the searing pain of realization took hold that something was wrong—that maybe you were not developing as quickly as your peers, and then when we understood that it was more serious than that. I loved you when we went from hospital to clinic to doctor looking for a medical diagnosis that would bring some hope. And, of course, we always prayed for you—and prayed, and prayed. I loved you when one of the tests resulted in too much spinal fluid being drawn from your body and you screamed. I loved you when you moaned and cried, when your mom and I and your sisters would drive for hours late at night to help you fall asleep. I loved you with tears in my eyes when, confused, you would bite your fingers or your lip by accident, and when your eyes crossed and then went blind.

I most certainly loved you when you could no longer speak, but how profoundly I missed your voice! I loved you when your scoliosis started wrenching your body like a pretzel, when we put a tube in your stomach so you could eat because you were choking on your food, which we fed you one spoonful at a time for up to two hours per meal. I managed to love you when your contorted limbs would not allow ease of changing your messy diapers—so many diapers—ten years of diapers. Bristol, I even loved you when you could not say the one thing in life that I longed to hear back— "Daddy, I love you." Bristol, I loved you when I was close to God and when He seemed far away, when I was full of faith and also when I was angry at Him.

And the reason I loved you, my Bristol, in spite of these difficulties, is that God put this love in my heart. This is the wondrous nature of God's love, that he loves us even when we are blind, deaf or twisted—in body or in spirit. God loves us even when we can't tell Him that we love Him back.

My dear Bristol, now you are free! I look forward to that day, according to God's promises, when we will be joined together with you with the Lord, completely whole and full of joy. I'm so happy that you have your crown first. We will follow you someday in His time.

Before you were born I prayed for you. In my heart I knew that you would be an angel. And so you were!

Love, Daddy.

Though I have never met this loving father, I personally identify with the passion of his heart. What an understatement. I can still hardly read his words without fighting back tears.

The Juggler

Billy Graham
Retold by Alice Gray

He was born in Italy but came to the United States as a young man. He studied juggling and became famous throughout the whole world.

Finally he decided to retire. He longed to return to his home country and settle down. He took all his worldly possessions, booked a passage on a ship to Italy and invested all the rest of the money in a single diamond. He hid the diamond in his stateroom.

While aboard ship, he was showing a boy how he could juggle a bunch of apples. Soon a crowd had gathered. The pride of the moment went to his head. He ran to his stateroom and got the diamond. He explained to the crowd that it represented his entire life's savings. He started juggling the diamond. Soon he was taking more and more chances.

At one point he threw the diamond high into the air and the crowd gasped. Knowing what the diamond meant, they begged him not to do it again. Moved by the excitement of the moment, he threw the diamond even higher. Again the crowed gasped and then sighed in relief when he caught the diamond.

Having total confidence in himself and his ability, the juggler told the crowd he would throw it up one more time. This time it would be so high that it would be out of sight for a moment. Again, they begged him not to do it.

But with the confidence of all his years of experience, he threw the diamond high into the air. It actually did disappear for a moment. Then the diamond returned into view sparkling in the sunlight. At that moment, the ship lurched and the diamond dropped into the sea and was lost forever.

We all feel terrible about the man's loss of all his worldly possessions. But God compares our soul as more valuable than the possessions of the whole world.

Just like the man in the story, some of us are juggling with our souls. We trust in ourselves and our own ability and the fact that we have gotten by before. Oftentimes there are people around us begging us to stop taking the risk because they recognize the value of our soul.

But we continue to juggle one more time...never knowing when the ship will lurch and we will have lost our chance forever.

The Tale of Three Trees

A traditional folktale
Retold by Angela Elwell Hunt

Once upon a mountaintop, three little trees stood and dreamed of what they wanted to become when they grew up.

The first little tree looked up at the stars twinkling like diamonds above him. "I want to hold treasure," he said. "I want to be covered with gold and filled with precious stones. I will be the most beautiful treasure chest in the world!"

The second little tree looked out at the small stream trickling by on its way to the ocean. "I want to be a strong sailing ship," he said. "I want to travel mighty waters and carry powerful kings. I will be the strongest ship in the world!"

The third little tree looked down into the valley below where busy men and busy women worked in a busy town. "I don't want to leave this mountaintop at all," she said. "I want to grow so tall that when people stop to look at me they will raise their eyes to heaven and think of God. I will be the tallest tree in the world!"

Years passed. The rains came, the sun shone, and the little trees grew tall.

One day three woodcutters climbed the mountain.

The first woodcutter looked at the first tree and said, "This tree is beautiful. It is perfect for me." With a swoop of his shining axe, the first tree fell.

"Now I shall be made into a beautiful chest," thought the first tree. "I shall hold wonderful treasure."

The second woodcutter looked at the second tree and said, "This tree is strong. It is perfect for me." With a swoop of his shining axe, the second tree fell.

"Now I shall sail mighty waters," thought the second tree. "I shall be a strong ship fit for kings!"

The third tree felt her heart sink when the last woodcutter looked her way. She stood straight and tall and pointed bravely to heaven.

But the woodcutter never even looked up. "Any kind of tree will do for me," he muttered. With a swoop of his shining axe, the third tree fell.

The first tree rejoiced when the woodcutter brought him to a carpenter's shop, but the busy carpenter was not thinking about treasure chests. Instead his work-worn hands fashioned the tree into a feed box for animals.

The once-beautiful tree was not covered with gold or filled with treasure. He was coated with sawdust and filled with hay for hungry farm animals.

The second tree smiled when the woodcutter took him to a shipyard, but no mighty sailing ships were being made that day. Instead the once-strong tree was hammered and sawed into a simple fishing boat.

Too small and too weak to sail an ocean or even a river, he was taken to a little lake. Every day he brought in loads of dead, smelly fish.

The third tree was confused when the woodcutter cut her into strong beams and left her in a lumberyard.

"What happened?" the once-tall tree wondered. "All I ever wanted to do was stay on the mountaintop and point to God."

Many, many days and nights passed. The three trees nearly forgot their dreams.

But one night golden starlight poured over the first tree as a young woman placed her newborn baby in the feed box.

"I wish I could make a cradle for him," her husband whispered.

The mother squeezed his hand and smiled as the starlight shone on the smooth and sturdy wood. "This manger is beautiful," she said.

And suddenly the first tree knew he was holding the greatest treasure in the world.

One evening a tired traveller and his friends crowded into the old fishing boat. The traveller fell asleep as the second tree quietly sailed out into the lake.

Soon a thrashing storm arose. The little tree shuddered. He knew he did not have the strength to carry so many passengers safely through the wind and rain.

The tired man awakened. He stood up, stretched out his hand, and said, "Peace." The storm stopped as quickly as it had begun.

And suddenly the second tree knew he was carrying the King of heaven and earth.

One Friday morning, the third tree was startled when her beams were yanked from the forgotten woodpile. She flinched as she was carried through an angry, jeering crowd. She shuddered when soldiers nailed a man's hands to her.

She felt ugly and harsh and cruel.

But on Sunday morning, when the sun rose and the earth trembled with joy beneath her, the third tree knew that God's love had changed everything.

It had made the first tree beautiful.

It had made the second tree strong.

And every time people thought of the third tree, they would think of God.

That was better than being the tallest tree in the whole world.

The Parable of Extravagant Love

Lloyd John Ogilvie
Chaplain of the United States Senate

A man had two sons. When the younger told his father, "I want my share of your estate now, instead of waiting until you die!" his father agreed to divide his wealth between his sons.

A few days later this younger son packed all his belongings and took a trip to a distant land, and there wasted all his money on parties and prostitutes. About the time his money was gone a great famine swept over the land, and he began to starve. He persuaded a local farmer to hire him to feed his pigs. The boy became so hungry that even the pods he was feeding the swine looked good to him. And no one gave him anything.

When he finally came to his senses, he said to himself, "At home even the hired men have food enough and to spare, and here I am dying of hunger! I will go home to my father and say, 'Father, I have sinned against both heaven and you, and am no longer worthy of being called your son. Please take me on as a hired man.'"

So he returned home to his father. And while he was still a long distance away, his father saw him coming, and was filled with loving pity and ran and embraced him and kissed him.

His son said to him, "Father, I have sinned against heaven and you, and am not worthy of being called your son—"

But his father said to the slaves, "Quick! Bring the finest robe in the house and put it on him. And a jeweled ring for his finger; and shoes! And kill the calf we have in the fattening pen. We must celebrate with a feast, for this son of mine was dead and has returned to life. He was lost and is found." So the party began.

Meanwhile, the older son was in the fields working; when he returned home, he heard dance music coming from the house, and he asked one of the servants what was going on.

*"Your brother is back," he was told, "and your father has killed
the calf we were fattening and has prepared a great feast to celebrate his coming home again unharmed."*

*The older brother was angry and wouldn't go in. His father
came out and begged him, but he replied, "All these years I've
worked hard for you and never once refused to do a single thing you
told me to; and in all that time you never gave me even one young
goat for a feast with my friends.*

*"Yet when this son of yours comes back after spending your
money on prostitutes, you celebrate by killing the finest calf we
have on the place."*

*"Look, dear son," his father said to him, "you and I are very
close, and everything I have is yours. But it is right to celebrate.
For he is your brother; and he was dead and has come back to life!
He was lost and is found!"*

A parable of Jesus
Luke 15:11–32 (TLB)

Now the parable tells us what kind of prodigal love awaits
us each time, every time, we return to the Father. He has been
waiting, watching, longing for us. Behold your God! This is
our God who sees His son a long way off and runs to meet
Him. Jesus' picture of the father running down the hill to
greet his son implies more than meets first glance. It was considered very undignified for a senior man to run. Aristotle
expressed the same Shibboleth: "Great men never run in public." But look at prodigal love give wings to the father's feet.
He can't run fast enough; his legs won't respond quickly
enough to express the expectant longing of his heart to welcome his son home.

Whatever else you believe about God, don't miss this. He
runs to us. Our least response unleashes His immense, incalcu-
lable responsiveness. Right now your God and mine is running to us to meet us and enfold us in His arms!

One Solitary Life

Author unknown

He was born in an obscure village, the child of a peasant woman. He grew up in still another village, where he worked in a carpenter shop until he was thirty. Then for three years he was an intinerant preacher.

He never wrote a book.

He never held an office.

He never had a family or owned a house.

He didn't go to college.

He never traveled 200 miles from the place where he was born. He did none of these things one usually associates with greatness.

He had no credentials but himself.

He was only 33 when public opinion turned against him. His friends ran away. He was turned over to his enemies and went through the mockery of a trial. He was nailed to a cross between two thieves.

When he was dying, his executioners gambled for his clothing, the only property he had on earth. When he was dead, he was laid in a borrowed grave through the pity of a friend.

Nineteen centuries have come and gone, and today he is the central figure of the human race, the leader of mankind's progress.

All the armies that ever marched, all the navies that ever sailed, all the parliaments that ever sat, all the kings that ever reigned, put together, have not affected the life of man on earth as much as that One Solitary Life.

Cecil B. De Mille

Billy Graham

Cecil B. De Mille once told me that his picture *The King of Kings*, made during the silent-movie era, was seen by an estimated 800,000,000 people. I asked him why he did not reproduce *The King of Kings* with sound and color. He replied, "I will never be able to do it, because if I gave Jesus a southern accent, the northerners would not think of Him as their Christ. If I gave Him a foreign accent, the Americans and the British would not think of Him as their Christ." He said, "As it is, people of all nations, from every race, creed, clan, can accept Him as their Christ."

Object Lesson

John MacArthur

A pastor went to see a man who didn't attend church very faithfully. The man was sitting before a fire, watching the warm glow of the coals. It was a cold winter day, but the coals were red hot, and the fire was warm. The pastor pleaded with the man to be more faithful in meeting with the people of God, but the man didn't seem to be getting the message.

So the pastor took the tongs beside the fireplace, pulled open the screen, and reached in and began to separate all the coals. When none of the coals was touching the others, he stood and watched in silence. In a matter of moments, they were all cold.... The man got the message.

Right on Time

Ron Mehl

Roger Simms had just left the military and was anxious to take his uniform off once and for all. He was hitchhiking home, and his heavy duffel bag made the trip even more arduous than hitchhiking normally is. Flashing his thumb to an oncoming car, he lost hope when he saw that it was a shiny, black, expensive car, so new that it had a temporary license in the back window...hardly the type of car that would stop for a hitchhiker.

But to his amazement, the car stopped and the passenger door opened. He ran toward the car, placed his duffel carefully in the back, and slid into the leather-covered front seat. He was greeted by the friendly smile of a handsome older gentleman with distinguished gray hair and a deep tan.

"Hello, son. Are you on leave or are you going home for good?"

"I just got out of the army, and I'm going home for the first time in several years," answered Roger.

"Well, you're in luck if you're going to Chicago," smiled the man.

"Not quite that far," said Roger, "but my home is on the way. Do you live there, Mister?"

"Hanover. Yes, I have a business there." And with that, they were on their way.

After giving each other brief life histories, and talking about everything under the sun, Roger (who was a Christian) felt a strong compulsion to witness to Mr. Hanover about Christ. But witnessing to an elderly, wealthy businessman who obviously had everything he could ever want was a scary prospect indeed. Roger kept putting it off, but as he neared his destination, he realized that it was now or never.

"Mr. Hanover," began Roger, "I would like to talk to you

about something very important." He then proceeded to explain the way of salvation, ultimately asking Mr. Hanover if he would like to receive Christ as his Savior. To Roger's astonishment, the big car pulled over to the side of the road; Roger thought for a moment that Mr. Hanover was about to throw him out. Then a strange and wonderful thing happened: the businessman bowed his head to the steering wheel and began to cry, affirming that he did in fact want to accept Christ into his heart. He thanked Roger for talking to him, saying that, "This is the greatest thing that has ever happened to me." He then dropped Roger at his house and traveled on toward Chicago.

Five years went by, and Roger Simms married, had a child, and started a business of his own. One day, while packing for a business trip to Chicago, he came across a small, gold-embossed business card which Mr. Hanover had given him years earlier.

When Roger arrived in Chicago, he looked up Hanover Enterprises, and found it to be located downtown in a very tall and important-looking building. The receptionist told him that it would be impossible to see Mr. Hanover, but that if he was an old friend, he would be able to see Mrs. Hanover. A little disappointed, he was led into a poshly-decorated office where a woman in her fifties was sitting at a huge oak desk.

She extended her hand. "You knew my husband?"

Roger explained how Mr. Hanover had been kind enough to give him a ride back home.

A look of interest passed across her face. "Can you tell me what date that was?"

"Sure," said Roger. "It was May 7th, five years ago, the day I was discharged from the army."

"And did anything special happen on your ride...anything unusual?"

Roger hesitated. Should he mention giving his witness?

Had it been some source of contention between the two, which resulted in a marital breakup or separation? But once again, he felt the prompting of the Lord to be truthful. "Mrs. Hanover, your husband accepted the Lord into his heart that day. I explained the gospel message to him, and he pulled to the side of the road and wept, and then chose to pray a prayer of salvation."

Suddenly, she began to sob uncontrollably. After several minutes, she regained enough control to explain what had happened: "I grew up in a Christian home, but my husband did not. I had prayed for my husband's salvation for many years, and I believed God would save him. But just after he let you out of his car, on May 7th, he passed away in a horrible head-on collision. He never arrived home. I thought God had not kept His promise, and I stopped living for the Lord five years ago because I blamed Him for not keeping His word."

I can identify with Mrs. Hanover. Perhaps you can, too. There are long, lonely stretches in life when it seems as if God has simply become indifferent toward our plight and bored or apathetic about our fervent prayers.

It's like staring at tightly wrapped, mysterious, and unavailable presents under a tree. As time goes on and hope stretches thin, we begin to wonder if God really has any gifts for us.

Maybe you've been waiting a long time for situations to change in your life. You've been waiting for a change in your health, in your relationships, in your spouse, in your children, in your job, in your finances, in your spiritual life. And it seems the delay goes on forever. It seems Christmas will never come. It seems the light will never change. It seems you've dialed the Lord's 9-1-1 line a thousand times and He's never answered.

Mary and Martha know all about that. They watched their brother weaken and fail. His life slipped though their fingers like sand and they couldn't stop it and the Lord didn't come.

But then He did come. And it was too late. But it wasn't too late. Because what He had in mind was something so far beyond their thoughts and experience and hopes and dreams that they didn't even think to ask for it.

It was a Very Good Thing wrapped in a Very Bad Thing.

And He delivered it Himself...right on time.

He always does.

Jump

Retold by Tania Gray

After the long day at work in his cubicle, the young man simply wanted to go home, relax, and prepare for his next day at work. As he made his way toward the elevator, he heard screaming and saw black smoke and flames billowing out of the hallway. Panic gripped him as a succession of thoughts flew through his mind, *I'm on the sixth floor. I'll never make it down. I'm going to die!* What he considered to be his only escape—the hallway—was engulfed in flames and impossible to navigate. As his mind continued to race, he heard fire engines and remembered that the office was lined with tall windows all across his floor. He coughed and staggered to the windows in hope of a swift rescue. Instead, when he looked down he could see nothing but a curtain of smoke covering the area. Through the smoke and flames, he realized that a crowd had gathered and along with the firemen everyone was yelling, "Jump!" "Jump!" The young man felt a cloud of fear envelop him. Over a loudspeaker he heard the voice of what he assumed to be a fireman, "The only way you'll survive is if you jump. We've spread out a safety net. You'll be perfectly safe." As the crowd continued to yell, the young man realized he didn't have the courage to make the leap without being able to see the net. His feet were cemented to the floor. Then, over the loudspeaker came the voice of his dad, "It's okay son, you can jump." As the familiar voice reached the young man, he felt the grip of fear lift. The trust and love that had been established between dad and son gave him the courage to jump safely down into the net.

Do we know and trust our heavenly Father's love that much?

Appointment with Death

Sermon illustration used by Peter Marshall
Retold by Alice Gray

There is an old legend about a rich merchant in Baghdad who sent his servant to the market. While he was at the marketplace, he was jostled by someone in the crowd. When he turned around he saw a woman in a long black cloak and knew it was Death. The servant ran home to his master and in a trembling voice told him about the encounter and how Death had looked at him and made a threatening gesture.

The servant begged his master to loan him a horse so he could ride to Samarra and hide so Death would not find him. The master agreed and the servant galloped away.

Later the merchant went down to the marketplace and saw Death standing nearby. The merchant asked, "Why did you make a threatening gesture to my servant and frighten him?" "That was not a threatening gesture" Death replied. "It was just that I was startled to see him in Baghdad because I have an appointment with him tonight in Samarra!"

The Story of the Praying Hands

Author unknown

About 1490 two young friends, Albrecht Dürer and Franz Knigstein, were struggling young artists. Since both were poor, they worked to support themselves while they studied art.

Work took so much of their time and advancement was slow. Finally, they reached an agreement: they would draw lots, and one of them would work to support both of them while the other would study art. Albrecht won and began to study, while Franz worked at hard labor to support them. They agreed that when Albrecht was successful he would support Franz who would then study art.

Albrecht went off to the cities of Europe to study. As the world now knows, he had not only talent but genius. When he had attained success, he went back to keep his bargain with Franz. But Albrecht soon discovered the enormous price his friend had paid. For as Franz worked at hard manual labor to support his friend, his fingers had become stiff and twisted. His slender, sensitive hands had been ruined for life. He could no longer execute the delicate brush strokes necessary to fine painting. Though his artistic dreams could never be realized, he was not embittered but rather rejoiced in his friend's success.

One day Dürer came upon his friend unexpectedly and found him kneeling with his gnarled hands intertwined in prayer, quietly praying for the success of his friend although he himself could no longer be an artist. Albrecht Dürer, the great genius, hurriedly sketched the folded hands of his faithful friend and later completed a truly great masterpiece known as "The Praying Hands."

Today art galleries everywhere feature Albrecht Dürer's works, and this particular masterpiece tells an eloquent story of love, sacrifice, labor and gratitude. It has reminded multitudes world around of how they may also find comfort, courage and strength.

Learning 'bout Prayer

Howard Hendricks

He came to know the Lord on a Thursday evening, and on Sunday he showed up at church. The pastor announced that we were going to have an evening service, and of course the guy didn't know enough to stay home. So he showed up again. That's when he learned that our church had a Bible study and prayer meeting on Wednesday night, so he came that evening as well.

I sat next to him at the prayer meeting, and just before we got started, he turned to me and asked, "Do you think they'd mind if I prayed?"

"Of course not," I reassured him. "That's what we're here for."

"Yeah, I know," he said, "but I've got a problem. I can't pray the way you people do."

I told him, "That's no problem, friend. You should thank God for that!"

Well, we started praying, and I could tell he was too nervous to take part. Finally, I put my hand on his thigh to encourage him. I'll never forget his prayer: "Lord, this is Jim," he began. "I'm the one who met you last Thursday night? I'm sorry, Lord, because I can't say it the way the rest of these people do, but I want to tell you the best I know how. I love you, Lord. I really do. Thanks a lot. I'll see you later."

I tell you, that prayer ignited our prayer meeting! Some of us had been doing a good job of talking about theology in prayer—you know, exploring the universe of doctrine, scraping the Milky Way with our big words. But this guy prayed—earnestly!

My children have taught me many things about theology. When they were quite young, we had a scholar visiting our home. After our meal, we were ready for our customary time of family worship, and we invited the man to join us. When it came time to pray, the kids, in typical childlike fashion, thanked Jesus for the tricycle and the sandbox and the fence and so on. Our guest could scarcely wait to take me aside.

"Professor Hendricks," he began, very much the lecturer that he was, "you don't mean to tell me that you're a professor in a theological seminary, and yet you teach your children to pray for things like that?"

"I certainly do," I replied. "Do you ever pray about your Ford?" I knew he did. He had to: he was riding mostly on faith and frayed fabric!

"Of course," he replied, "but that's different."

"Oh, really?" I countered. "What makes you think your Ford is more important to God than my boy's tricycle?" Then I pressed him further. "You're on the road a lot. Do you ever pray for protection?"

"Brother Hendricks, I never go anywhere but that I pray for the Lord's journeying mercies."

"Well, safety is essentially what my boy is thanking Jesus for when he thanks him for the fence. That fence keeps out those great big dogs on the other side!"

The Secret of the Gifts
Paul Flucke

The story has been told for centuries now—how Gaspar, Melchoir and Balthasar brought gifts to the newborn king. Ah, you say, everyone knows. They brought gold, frankincense and myrrh. So it has been told.

But the story is incomplete. Listen to the rest. You shall learn the secret of the gifts.

Those who watched saw the first of the three visitors pause at the door: Gaspar, a wealthy man with a cloak of fine velvet, trimmed in flawless fur. They could not see that it was the Angel Gabriel, guarding the holy place, before whom Gaspar stopped.

"All who enter must bring a gift," Gabriel told Gaspar.

Struggling to lift a finely wrought box, Gaspar said, "I have brought bars of the finest gold."

"Your gift," Gabriel said, "must be something of the essence of yourself, something precious to your soul."

"Such have I brought," Gaspar said.

But as he kneeled to lay his gold before the child, he stopped and stood erect. In his outstretched hand lay not gold, but a hammer. Its scarred and blackened head was larger than a man's fist; its handle, of sinewy wood, as long as a man's forearm. Gaspar stammered, dumbfounded.

The angel said softly, "What you hold in your hands is the hammer of your greed, used to pound wealth from those who labor so that you may live in luxury, to build a mansion for yourself while others dwell in hovels."

Gaspar bowed his head in shame and turned to leave. But Gabriel blocked the way: "No, you have not offered your gift."

"Give this?" Gaspar blurted in horror. "Not to a king!"

"This is why you came," Gabriel said. "You cannot take it back. It's too heavy. Leave it here or it will destroy you."

"Why, the child cannot lift it," Gaspar protested.

"He is the only one who can," replied the angel.

Next to step to the door was Melchoir, the scholar with the length of his beard and furrows of his brow to bespeak the wisdom of age. He, too, paused before the door.

"What have you brought?" asked Gabriel.

"Frankincense, the fragrance of hidden lands and bygone days," Melchoir replied.

"Your gift," cautioned Gabriel, "must be something precious to your soul."

Melchoir stood breathless, kneeling reverently down to draw from beneath his robe a silver flask. But the vessel in his hand was not silver at all. It was common clay, tough and stained. Aghast, he pulled the stopper from its mouth and sniffed the contents.

"This is vinegar!" Melchoir snarled.

"You have brought what you are made of," Gabriel said. "Bitterness. The soured wine of a life turned grim with jealousy and hate; carried within too long, the memory of old hurts, hoarded resentments, and smoldering anger. You have sought knowledge, but filled your life with poison."

Melchoir's shoulders drooped. Turning his face away, he fumbled to hide the earthen jar. Gabriel touched Melchoir's arm: "Wait, you must leave your gift."

Melchoir sighed with pain deep from within. "But this is vile stuff," he protested. "What if the child should touch it to his lips?"

"You must leave that worry to heaven," Gabriel replied. "There is use even for vinegar."

One more visitor strode forward: Balthasar, the leader of many legions and scourge of walled cities. He grasped a brass-bound box.

"I bring myrrh," he said, "the most precious booty of my boldest conquest. Many have fought and died for such as this, the essence of a most rare herb."

"But is it the essence of yourself?" Gabriel asked.

The soldier shuffled forward, bowing his head near the ground and releasing his grip on the handle of the box. But what he lay before the baby's feet was his own spear.

"It cannot be!" he whispered hoarsely. "Some enemy has cast a spell."

"That is more true than you know," Gabriel said from behind. "A thousand enemies have cast their spell on you and turned your soul into a spear. Living only to conquer, you have been conquered. Each battle you win leads only to another."

Balthasar grasped the weapon and turned to the door. "I cannot leave this."

"Are you sure?" Gabriel asked.

"But here?" the warrior whispered. "He is but a child. The spear could pierce his flesh."

"That fear you must leave to heaven," Gabriel replied.

What of the gifts you ask—the hammer, vinegar and spear. Another story tells how they were seen once more, years later, on a lonely hill outside Jerusalem. But do not worry. That is a burden heaven itself took care of as only heaven can.

Paraclete

David Seamands

I read the experience of a man who underwent open heart surgery. He said:

The day before the surgery an attractive nurse came into my room to visit. She took hold of my hand, and told me to feel it and hold it. I thought that was a great idea!

"Now," she said, "during the surgery tomorrow you will be disconnected from your heart and you will be kept alive only by virtue of certain machines. And when your heart is finally restored and the operation is over and you are recovering, you will eventually awaken in a special recovery room. But you will be immobile for as long as six hours. You may be unable to move, or speak, or even to open your eyes, but you will be perfectly conscious and you will hear and you will know everything that is going on around you. During those six hours I will be at your side and I will hold your hand, exactly as I am doing now. I will stay with you until you are fully recovered. Although you may feel absolutely helpless, when you feel my hand, you will know that I will not leave you."

It happened exactly as the nurse told me. I awoke, and could do nothing. But I could feel the nurse's hand in my hand for hours. And that made the difference!

Jesus' favorite word for His promised presence in the Holy Spirit is Paraclete—"the One called alongside." Engrave the words of Jesus on your mind until they will be such a part of you that during the lowest depression you will know, regardless of how you feel, that He is with you.

Selling Cattle
Howard Hendricks

Shortly after [Dallas] Seminary was founded in 1924, it almost folded. It came to the point of bankruptcy. All the creditors were ready to foreclose at twelve noon on a particular day. That morning, the founders of the school met in the president's office to pray that God would provide. In that prayer meeting was Harry Ironside. When it was his turn to pray, he said in his refreshingly candid way, "Lord, we know that the cattle on a thousand hills are Thine. Please sell some of them and send us the money."

Just about that time, a tall Texan in boots and an open-collar shirt strolled into the business office. "Howdy!" he said to the secretary. "I just sold two carloads of cattle over in Fort Worth. I've been trying to make a business deal go through, but it just won't work. I feel God wants me to give this money to the seminary. I don't know if you need it or not, but here's the check," and he handed it over.

The secretary took the check and, knowing something of the critical nature of the hour, went to the door of the prayer meeting and timidly tapped. Dr. Lewis Sperry Chafer, the founder and president of the school, answered the door and took the check from her hand. When he looked at the amount, it was for the exact sum of the debt. Then he recognized the name on the check as that of the cattleman. Turning to Dr. Ironside, he said, "Harry, God sold the cattle."

What If I Get Tired of Being In Heaven?

Larry Libby
(From a children's book)

If you are thinking you might get bored or tired after being in Heaven for a while...don't worry! Try to imagine something with me. Imagine you are a little bird who lives in a tiny cage made of rusty metal. And inside your cage you have a food dish, and a little mirror, and a tiny perch to swing on.

Then one day some kind person takes your cage to a big, beautiful forest. The forest is splashed with sunlight. Proud, towering trees cover the hills and valleys as far as you can see. There are gushing waterfalls, and bushes drooping with purple berries, and fruit trees, and carpets of wild flowers, and a wide blue sky to fly in. And besides all these things, there are millions of other little birds...

> hopping from one green limb to another
> > and eating their fill
> > > and raising their little families
> > > > and singing their hearts out
> > > > > all through the day.

Now, little bird, can you imagine wanting to stay in your cage? Can you imagine saying, "Oh please don't let me go. I will miss my cage. I will miss my little food dish with seeds in it. I will miss my plastic mirror and my tiny little perch. I might get bored in that big forest."

That would be silly, wouldn't it? And it's just as silly to think we might run out of things to do in Heaven!

My Heart, Christ's Home
Robert Boyd Munger

One evening I invited Jesus Christ into my heart. What an entrance He made! It was not a spectacular, emotional thing, but very real. Something happened at the very center of my life. He came into the darkness of my heart and turned on the light. He built a fire on the hearth and banished the chill. He started music where there had been stillness, and He filled the emptiness with His own loving, wonderful fellowship. I have never regretted opening the door to Christ and I never will.

In the joy of this new relationship I said to Jesus Christ, "Lord, I want this heart of mine to be Yours. I want to have You settle down here and be perfectly at home. Everything I have belongs to You. Let me show You around."

The Study
The first room was the study—the library. In my home this room of the mind is a very small room with very thick walls. But it is a very important room. In a sense, it is the control room of the house. He entered with me and looked around at the books in the bookcase, the magazines upon the table, the pictures on the walls. As I followed His gaze I became uncomfortable.

Strangely, I had not felt self-conscious about this before, but now that He was there looking at these things I was embarrassed. Some books were there that His eyes were too pure to behold. On the table were a few magazines that a Christian had no business reading. As for the pictures on the walls—the imaginations and thoughts of the mind—some of these were shameful.

Red-faced, I turned to Him and said, "Master, I know that this room needs to be cleaned up and made over. Will You help me make it what it ought to be?"

"Certainly!" He said, "I'm glad to help you. First of all, take all the things that you are reading and looking at which are not helpful, pure, good and true, and throw them out! Now put on the empty shelves the books of the Bible. Fill the library with Scripture and meditate on it day and night. As for the pictures on the walls, you will have difficulty controlling these images, but I have something that will help." He gave me of full-sized portrait of Himself. "Hang this centrally," He said, "on the wall of the mind."

I did, and I have discovered through the years that when my thoughts are centered upon Christ Himself, His purity and power cause impure thoughts to back away. So He has helped me to bring my thoughts under His control.

The Dining Room

From the study we went into the dining room, the room of appetites and desires. I spent a lot of time and hard work here trying to satisfy my wants.

I said to Him, "This is a favorite room. I am quite sure You will be pleased with what we serve."

He seated Himself at the table with me and asked, "What is on the menu for dinner?" "Well," I said, "my favorite dishes: money, academic degrees and stocks, with newspaper articles of fame and fortune as side dishes." These were the things I liked—secular fare.

When the food was placed before Him, He said nothing, but I observed that He did not eat it. I said to Him, "Master, don't You care for this food? What is the trouble?"

He answered, "I have food to eat that you do not know of. If you want food that really satisfies you, do the will of the Father. Stop seeking your own pleasures, desires, and satisfaction. Seek to please Him. The food will satisfy you."

There at the table He gave me a taste of the joy of doing

God's will. What flavor! There is no food like it in all the world. It alone satisfies.

The Living Room

From the dining room we walked into the living room. This room was intimate and comfortable. I liked it. It had a fireplace, overstuffed chairs, a sofa, and a quiet atmosphere.

He said, "This is indeed a delightful room. Let us come here often. It is secluded and quiet, and we can fellowship together."

Well, as a young Christian I was thrilled. I couldn't think of anything I would rather do than have a few minutes with Christ in close companionship.

He promised, "I will be here early every morning. Meet me here, and we will start the day together."

So morning after morning, I would come downstairs to the living room. He would take a book of the Bible from the case. We would open it and read together. He would unfold to me the wonder of God's saving truths. My heart sang as He shared the love and the grace He had toward me. These were wonderful times.

However, little by little, under the pressure of many responsibilities, this time began to be shortened. Why, I'm not sure. I thought I was too busy to spend regular time with Christ. This was not intentional, you understand. It just happened that way. Finally, not only was the time shortened, but I began to miss days now and then. Urgent matters would crowd out the quiet times of conversation with Jesus.

I remember one morning rushing downstairs, eager to be on my way. I passed the living room and noticed that the door was open.

Looking in, I saw a fire in the fireplace and Jesus was sitting there. Suddenly in dismay I thought to myself, "He is my guest. I invited Him into my heart! He has come as my Savior and Friend, and yet I am neglecting Him."

I stopped, turned and hesitantly went in. With downcast glance, I said, "Master, forgive me. Have You been here all these mornings?"

"Yes," He said, "I told you I would be here every morning to meet with you. Remember, I love you. I have redeemed you at great cost. I value your fellowship. Even if you cannot keep the quiet time for your own sake, do it for mine."

The truth that Christ desires my companionship, that He wants me to be with Him and waits for me, has done more to transform my quiet time with God than any other single fact. Don't let Christ wait alone in the living room of your heart, but every day find time when, with your Bible and in prayer, you may be together with Him.

The Workroom

Before long, He asked, "Do you have a workroom in your home?" Out in the garage of the home of my heart I had a workbench and some equipment, but I was not doing much with it. Once in a while I would play around with a few little gadgets, but I wasn't producing anything substantial.

I led Him out there. He looked over the workbench and said, "Well, this is quite well furnished. What are you producing with your life for the Kingdom of God?" He looked at one or two little toys that I had thrown together on the bench and held one up to me. "Is this the sort of thing you are doing for others in your Christian life?"

"Well," I said, "Lord, I know it isn't much, and I really want to do more, but after all, I don't seem to have strength or skill to do more."

"Would you like to do better?" He asked.

"Certainly," I replied.

"All right. Let me have your hands. Now relax in me and let my Spirit work through you. I know that you are unskilled, clumsy and awkward, but the Holy Spirit is the Master Workman, and if He controls your hands and your heart, He will work through you." Stepping around behind me and putting His great, strong hands under mine, He held the tools in His skilled fingers and began to work through me. The more I relaxed and trusted Him, the more He was able to do with my life.

The Rec Room

He asked me if I had a rec room where I went for fun and fellowship. I was hoping He would not ask about that. There were certain associations and activities that I wanted to keep for myself.

One evening when I was on my way out with some of my buddies, He stopped me with a glance and asked, "Are you going out?"

I replied, "Yes."

"Good," He said, "I would like to go with you."

"Oh," I answered rather awkwardly. "I don't think, Lord Jesus, that You would really enjoy where we are going. Let's go out together tomorrow night. Tomorrow night we will go to a Bible class at church, but tonight I have another appointment."

"I'm sorry," He said. "I thought that when I came into your home, we were going to do everything together, to be close companions. I just want you to know that I am willing to go with you."

"Well," I mumbled, slipping out the door, "we will go someplace together tomorrow night."

That evening I spent some miserable hours. I felt rotten. What kind of friend was I to Jesus, deliberately leaving Him out of my life, doing things and going places that I knew very well He would not enjoy?

When I returned that evening, there was a light in His

room, and I went up to talk it over with Him. I said, "Lord, I have learned my lesson. I know now that I can't have a good time without You. From now on, we will do everything together."

Then we went down into the rec room of the house. He transformed it. He brought new friends, new excitement, new joys. Laughter and music have been ringing through the house ever since.

The Hall Closet

One day I found Him waiting for me at the door. An arresting look was in His eye. As I entered, He said to me, "There is a peculiar odor in the house. Something must be dead around here. It's upstairs. I think it is in the hall closet."

As soon as He said this, I knew what He was talking about. There was a small closet up there on the hall landing, just a few feet square. In that closet, behind lock and key, I had one or two little personal things that I did not want anyone to know about. Certainly, I did not want Christ to see them. I knew they were dead and rotting things left over from my old life. I wanted them so for myself that I was afraid to admit they were there.

Reluctantly, I went up with Him, and as we mounted the stairs the odor became stronger and stronger. He pointed to the door. I was angry. That's the only way I can put it. I had given Him access to the library, the dining room, the living room, the workroom, the rec room, and now He was asking me about a little two-by-four closet. I said to myself, "This is too much. I am not going to give Him the key."

"Well," He said, reading my thoughts, "if you think I'm going to stay up here on the second floor with this smell, you are mistaken. I will go out on the porch." Then I saw Him start down the stairs.

When one comes to know and love Christ, the worst thing

that can happen is to sense Him withdrawing His fellowship. I had to give in.

"I'll give you the key," I said sadly, "but You will have to open the closet and clean it out I haven't the strength to do it."

"Just give me the key," He said. "Authorize me to take care of that closet and I will."

With trembling fingers I passed the key to Him. He took it, walked over to the door, opened it, entered, took out all the putrefying stuff that was rotting there, and threw it away. Then He cleaned the closet and painted it. It was done in a moment's time. Oh, what victory and release to have that dead thing out of my life!

Transferring the Title

A thought came to me. "Lord, is there any chance that You would take over the management of the whole house and operate it for me as You did that closet? Would You take the responsibility to keep my life what it ought to be?"

His face lit up as He replied, "I'd love to! That is what I want to do. You cannot be a victorious Christian in your own strength. Let me do it through you and for you. That is the way. But, He added slowly, "I am just a guest. I have no authority to proceed, since the property is not mine."

Dropping to my knees, I said, "Lord, You have been a guest and I have been the host. From now on I am going to be the servant. You are going to be the owner and Master."

Running as fast as I could to the strongbox, I took out the title deed to the house describing its assets and liabilities, location and situation. I eagerly signed the house over to Him alone for time and eternity. "Here," I said, "here it is, all that I am and have, forever. Now You run the house. I'll just remain with You as a servant and friend."

Things are different since Jesus Christ has settled down and has made His home in my heart.

Footprints
Margaret Fishback Powers

One night I had a dream. I dreamed I was walking along the beach with the Lord and across the sky flashed scenes from my life. For each scene I noticed two sets of footprints in the sand. One belonged to me and the other to the Lord.

When the last scene of my life flashed before us I looked back at the footprints in the sand. I noticed that many times along the path of my life there was only one set of footprints. I also noticed that it happened at the very lowest and saddest times in my life.

This really bothered me and I questioned the Lord about it. "Lord, you said that once I decided to follow You, You would walk with me all the way. But I noticed that during the most troublesome times in my life there was only one set of footprints. I don't understand why, in times when I needed You most, You should leave me."

The Lord replied, "My precious, precious child. I love you and I would never, never leave you during your times of trial and suffering. When you saw only one set of footprints…it was then that I carried you!"

The Applause of Heaven
Max Lucado

You'll be home soon, too. You may not have noticed it, but you are closer to home than ever before. Each moment is a step taken. Each breath is a page turned. Each day is a mile marked, a mountain climbed. You are closer to home than you've ever been.

Before you know it, your appointed arrival time will come; you'll descend the ramp and enter the City. You'll see faces that are waiting for you. You'll hear your name spoken by those who love you. And, maybe, just maybe—in the back, behind the crowds—the One who would rather die than live without you will remove his pierced hands from his heavenly robe and...applaud.

Notes

If you would like to contribute stories for a
possible second edition of
STORIES FOR THE HEART
please send them to the following address:

Alice Gray
Questar Publishers, Inc.
Post Office Box 1720
Sisters, Oregon 97759

For each story, please give author's name and original source of story if
previously published. Also, your own name, address, and phone number. We will not be able to contact everyone who submits a story, but
will notify you if the story you submit is used. Manuscripts and photo-
copies cannot be returned.

I hope these stories have touched your heart and encouraged your soul.

The LORD bless you and keep you;
the LORD make his face shine upon you
and be gracious to you;
the LORD turn his face toward you
and give you peace.

Numbers 6:24–27 (NIV)

Stories included in this book were collected over a period of twenty years. Reasonable care has been taken to trace original ownership and, when necessary, obtain permission to reprint. Some stories have been retold when there was no clue of the story's origin.

If I have overlooked giving proper credit to anyone, please contact Questar Publishers, Inc., Post Office Box 1720, Sisters, Oregon 97759 and corrections will be made prior to additional editions.

Notes and acknowledgments are listed by story title in the order they appear in each section of the book. For permission to reprint copyrighted material, grateful acknowledgment is made to authors, publishers, and agents—and especially to Multnomah Books (a division of Questar Publishers, Inc.), Word, Inc. and Zondervan Publishing House.

COMPASSION

"Together" by Emery Nester, quoted from *DEPRESSION* (Multnomah Books, a division of Questar Publishers, Inc.). Used with permission.

"The Day Philip Joined the Group" by Paul Harvey, copyright 1992. Used with permission.

"A Song in the Dark" by Max Lucado from *GOD CAME NEAR* (Multnomah Books, a division of Questar Publishers, Inc., 1987). Used with permission.

"There's Always Something Left to Love" by Tony Campolo (*Expression*, June 1995). Used with permission.

"Belonging" by Paul Brand and Philip Yancey from *IN HIS IMAGE* (© 1984 by Paul Brand and Philip Yancey). Used by permission of Zondervan Publishing House.

"Really Winning" by Michael Broome, retold by Alice Gray from a speech he gave at an education conference in 1984.

"Courage" as it appeared in *MOMENTS OF CHRISTMAS* by Robert Strand (New Leaf Press, 1993). Original source unknown. Used by permission of Robert Strand.

"Humpty Dumpty Revisited" by Vic Pentz (The Wittenburg Door, 1972). Used by permission of the author.

"Lessons From a Young Nurse" by Rebecca Manley Pippert from *OUT OF THE SALTSHAKER & INTO THE WORLD* (© 1979 by InterVarsity Christian Fellowship of the USA). Part of the story taken from "Lady in 415," as told to Hope Warwick, *Campus Life* (May 1976). Used by permission of InterVarsity Press, P.O. Box 1400, Downers Grove, IL 60515.

"One" by Everett Hale. Quoted from *THE REBIRTH OF AMERICA* (The Arthur S. DeMoss Foundation, 1986).

"It Matters" by Jeff Ostrander (Frontlines newsletter about 1993). *Frontlines* is an education resource for the Pregnancy Resource Center in Grand Rapids, MI. Used by permission.

"Understanding Mercy" by Alice Gray. Taken from scant notes in my file on the attributes of God.

ENCOURAGEMENT

"Chosen" by Marie Curling. The author lives in England. Contact with the author is still being attempted as this goes to press.

"The First Robin" by William E. Barton from THE MILLIONAIRE AND THE SCRUBLADY (© 1990 by William E. Barton). Used by permission of Zondervan Publishing House.

"Don't Quit" by Charles R. Swindoll from GROWING STRONG IN THE SEASONS OF LIFE (© 1983 by Charles R. Swindoll, Inc.). Used by permission of Zondervan Publishing House.

"The Guest of the Maestro" by Max Lucado from WHEN GOD WHISPERS YOUR NAME (Word, Inc., Dallas, TX, 1994). Used by permission. All rights reserved.

"Jimmy Durante" by Tim Hansel from HOLY SWEAT (Word, Inc., Dallas, TX, 1987). Used by permission. All rights reserved.

"The Day Bart Simpson Prayed" by Lee Strobel from WHAT JESUS WOULD SAY (© 1994 by Lee Strobel). Used by permission of Zondervan Publishing House. Note from Alice Gray: This prayer by Bart Simpson is from Lee Strobel's fascinating book where he asks the question, "What would Jesus say to people like Rush Limbaugh, Michael Jordan, Madalyn Murray O'Hair and others?" Lee Strobel points out that even though Bart's prayer wasn't a perfect model, Jesus would probably find some things Bart did right—he prayed from his heart, admitted he wasn't a good kid, and thought of God as his friend. Of course, there were other things Bart would need help with. Most of all, the author makes the point that for a spike-haired little terror like Bart Simpson, it was a good beginning.

"At the Counter" by Paula Kirk, Editor (*Tapestry Magazine*; Walk Thru the Bible Ministries). Used by permission.

"All the Good Things" by Sister Helen P. Mrosla. The original story appeared in *Proteus*. Condensed in the October 1991 *Reader's Digest*. Used by permission of the author.

"The Hand" presented to an elementary school teacher. Source and author unknown.

"The Kiss" by Richard Selzer from MORTAL LESSONS. Used by permission.

"Changed Lives" by Tim Kimmel from LITTLE HOUSE ON THE FREEWAY (Multnomah Books, a division of Questar Publishers, Inc.). Used by permission.

"The Passerby" by Hester Tetreault. © 1993. Hester lives in St. Helens, OR and is a freelance writer. Used by permission.

"Just a Kid with Cerebral Palsey" by Tony Campolo (U, April/May 1988). Used by permission of author.

"Repeat Performance" by Nancy Spiegelberg. Used by permission of the author.

VIRTUES

"Act Medium" by Leslie B. Flynn from GREAT CHURCH FIGHTS (Victor Books, 1976).

"Valentines" by Dale Galloway from DREAM A NEW DREAM. (Tyndale House Publishers, Inc., Carol Stream, IL, 1975).

"Choosing" by Victor E. Frankl as quoted in MOTIVATION TO LAST A LIFE-TIME by Ted W. Engstrom (Daybreak Books, 1984).

"It's a Start" by Garry Smalley and John Trent from HOME REMEDIES (Multnomah Books, a division of Questar Publishers, Inc., 1991). Used by permission.

"What's It Like in Your Town?" as retold by Kris Gray. Copyright 1995. Used by permission. Idea adapted from a few notes in my object lessons file.

"The Experiment" as retold by Marilyn McAuley from an article by Catherine Marshall called, "My Experiment With Fault-Finding." Source of article unknown. Marilyn McAuley is a freelance writer and copyeditor living in Milwaukie, OR.

"It Really Didn't Matter" by Charles Colson from THE BODY (Word, Inc., Dallas, TX, 1992).

"Monuments" by Charles L. Allen from YOU ARE NEVER ALONE (Fleming H. Revell Company, a division of Baker Book House, Grand Rapids, MI, 1978). Used by permission.

"Chickens" as retold by Anne Paden from Jack London's WHITE FANG. Anne contributes articles for the newsletter of the Crisis Pregnancy Centers of the Portland Metro Area in Oregon. Used by permission.

"The Millionaire and the Scrublady" by William E. Barton from THE MILLION-AIRE AND THE SCRUBLADY (© 1990 by William E. Barton). Used by permission of Zondervan Publishing House.

"The Signal" as retold by Alice Gray. Taken from a familar story passed down from my mother and others.

"A Gift from the Heart" by Norman Vincent Peale (Reader's Digest, January 1968, © 1968). Reprinted with permission of the Reader's Digest Assn., Inc.

"Thankful in Everything?" by Matthew Henry. Excerpted from Our Daily Bread, month and year unknown.

"The Good Samaritan" by Tim Hansel from *HOLY SWEAT* (Word, Inc., Dallas, TX, 1987). Used by permission. All rights reserved.

"Contentment Is..." by Ruth Senter from *STARTLED BY SILENCE* (Zondervan Publishing House, 1986). Used by permission of author.

MOTIVATION

"Keeper of the Spring" by Charles R. Swindoll from *IMPROVING YOUR SERVE* (Word, Inc., Dallas, TX, 1981). Used with permission. All rights reserved.

"A Man Can't Just Sit Around" by Chip McGregor. Quoted from *STANDING TOGETHER* (Vision House Publishing, Inc., Gresham, OR, 1995). Used by permission. Chip is a freelance writer and editor who lives in the Portland, OR area.

"Come On, Get With It!" by Howard Hendricks from *TEACHING TO CHANGE LIVES* (Multnomah Books, a division of Questar Publisher, Inc., 1987). Used by permission.

"The Nearest Battle" by Richard C. Halverson. Used by permission.

"Mentoring" by Chip McGregor. From the book *STANDING TOGETHER* (Vision House Publishing, Inc., Gresham, OR, 1995). Used by permission.

"Success" retold by Alice Gray. An illustration heard many years ago. Source unknown.

"The Red Umbrella" retold by Tania Gray. © 1995. Used by permission. Idea adapted from a few notes in my object lesson file.

"All It Takes is a Little Motivation" by Zig Ziglar from *OVER THE TOP* (Thomas Nelson Publishers, 1994). Used by permission.

"An Autobiography in Five Short Paragraphs" by Portia Nelson.

"Beautiful Day, Isn't It?" by Barbara Johnson from *FRESH ELASTIC FOR STRETCHED OUT MOMS* (Fleming H. Revell, 1986).

"Don't Give Up..." retold by Alice Gray. Adapted from a Focus on the Family radio broadcast.

"Make Up Your Mind, Oreo!" by Arthur Gordon. Source unknown.

"Head-Hunter" by Josh McDowell from *BUILDING YOUR SELF IMAGE* (Living Books, a division of Tyndale House Publishers, 1986).

"If I Had My Life to Live Over" by Brother Jeremiah. Source unknown. Quoted from *FRESH ELASTIC FOR STRETCHED OUT MOMS* (Fleming H. Revell, 1986).

LOVE

"The Gift of the Magi" by O. Henry. Public Domain.

"Believing in Each Other" by Steve Stephens, adapted from MARRIAGE: EXPERI-ENCE THE BEST (Vision House Publishing, Inc., Gresham, OR., 1995). Used by permission.

"Act of Love" from MIRROR, MIRROR by Alice Gray and Marilyn McAuley (Zondervan Publishing House, 1986).

"Come Home" by Max Lucado from NO WONDER THEY CALL HIM SAVIOR (Multnomah Books, a division of Questar Publishers, Inc., 1986). Used by permission.

FAMILY

"Someday" by Charles R. Swindoll from COME BEFORE WINTER (© 1985 by Charles R. Swindoll, Inc.). Used by permission of Zondervan Publishing House.

"Longer, Daddy, Longer..." by John Trent from LEAVING THE LIGHTS ON by Gary Smalley and John Trent (Multnomah Books, a division of Questar Publishers, Inc., 1994). Used by permission.

"Balloons" by James Dobson from PARENTING ISN'T FOR COWARDS (Word, Inc., Dallas, TX, 1987). Note from Alice Gray: Dr. Dobson told this story as a word of encouragement to parents of every low-flying kid in the world today. He went on to say that he wishes he could put his arm around you and let you know he under-stands your pain and fears. He believes parents today are much too willing to blame themselves for everything their children or adolescents do...especially those parents who give a high priority to their family. I hope you will read his book and feel the tenderness he has for parents whose children have not yet soared.

"What's a Grandmother?" (Author and source unknown). Given to me by an ele-mentary school teacher. Also quoted in WHAT WIVES WISH THEIR HUS-BANDS KNEW ABOUT WOMEN by James Dobson (Tyndale House, 1975).

"The Wall" (Author unknown). Quoted from IT'S WHO YOU KNOW by David Simpson (Vision House Publishing, Inc., Gresham, OR., 1995).

"Soft Touch" by James Dobson from LOVE FOR A LIFETIME (Multnomah Books, a division of Questar Publishers, Inc., 1993). Used by permission.

"When You Thought I Wasn't Looking" (Author unknown) quoted from LEARN-ING TO LOVE WHEN LOVE ISN'T EASY (Victor Books, 1992).

"Growing Up" by Marilyn K. McAuley, © 1995. Used by permission. Marilyn is a freelance writer and copyeditor living in Milwaukie, OR.

"Even If It's Dark" by Ron Mehl from GOD WORKS THE NIGHT SHIFT (Multnomah Books, a division of Questar Publishers, Inc., 1994). Used by permis-sion.

"Got a Minute?" by David Jeremiah from ACTS OF LOVE (Vision House Publishing, Inc., Gresham, OR, 1994). Used by permission.

LIFE

"Kennedy's Question" by Billy Graham from *BILLY GRAHAM: THE INSPIRATIONAL WRITINGS* (Word, Inc., Dallas, TX, 1995). Used by permission. All rights reserved.

"If We Had Hurried" by Billy Rose as quoted in *COME BEFORE WINTER* by Charles R. Swindoll (Zondervan Publishing House, 1985). Used by permission.

"Spring Filly" by Nancy Spiegelberg. Used by permission of author.

"The Hammer, The File, and The Furnace" by Charles R. Swindoll from *COME BEFORE WINTER* (© 1985 by Charles R. Swindoll, Inc.). Used by permission of Zondervan Publishing House.

"Three Men and a Bridge" by Sandy Snavely, copyright 1995. Used by permission. Sandy is a retreat speaker and Christian radio talk show host in Portland, OR.

"Incredible!" by David Jeremiah from *Power of Encouragement* (Multnomah Books, a division of Questar Publishers, Inc., Sisters, OR, 1994). Used by permission.

"Struggles" retold by Alice Gray. A favorite story heard in a variety of settings throughout the years. I like to use it when teaching on endurance in the tough times.

"He Listened" by Joseph Bayly as quoted in *Power of Encouragement* by David Jeremiah (Multnomah Books, a division of Questar Publishers, Inc., Sisters, OR, 1994).

"Do You Wish to Get Well?" by Kay Arthur from *MY SAVIOR, MY FRIEND* (Harvest House Publishers, 1995). Used by permission of Precept Ministries.

"Heritage" by Sally J. Knower, copyright 1995. Used by permission. Sally is a freelance writer living in Milwaukie, OR.

"The Orchestra" by Judy Urschel Straalsund, © 1987. Used by permission. Judy is a freelance writer and artistic director of Tapestry Theatre in Portland, OR.

"Do You Know Who His Daddy Is?" by Zig Ziglar from *OVER THE TOP* (Thomas Nelson Publishers, 1994). Used by permission.

"Let Go" by Billy Graham from *BILLY GRAHAM: THE INSPIRATIONAL WRITINGS* (Word, Inc., Dallas, TX, 1995). Used by permission. All rights reserved.

"Runaways" by Cliff Schimmels from *LESSONS FROM THE GOOD OLD DAYS* (Victor Books, 1994). Used by permission.

"Significance" by Joni Eareckson Tada from *GLORIOUS INTRUDER* (Multnomah Books, a division of Questar Publishers, Inc., 1989). Used by permission.

"Somebody Loved Him" by Rebecca Manley Pippert from *HOPE HAS ITS REASONS* (HarperSan Francisco a Division of HarperCollins Publishers, 1989). Used by permission.

"Homecoming" by Michael Broome, retold by Alice Gray from a speech he gave at an education conference in 1984.

"Picture of Peace" by Catherine Marshall from FRIENDS WITH GOD (Fleming H. Revell, 1956). Used by permission.

FAITH

"Where Do You Run?" by Kay Arthur from TO KNOW HIM BY NAME (Mulnomah Books, a division of Questar Publishers, Inc., 1995). Used by permission.

"Dear Bristol" by James Dobson from WHEN GOD DOESN'T MAKE SENSE (© 1993 by Tyndale House Publishers, Inc.). Used by permission. All rights reserved.

"The Juggler" by Billy Graham, retold by Alice Gray from illustration heard on a television broadcast of a Billy Graham crusade in the 1980s.

"The Tale of Three Trees" the retelling of a traditional folkstale by Angela Elwell Hunt (Lion Publishing, Colorado Springs, CO, 1989). Used by permission. Memo from Alice: Text is from a beautiful illustrated gift book.

"The Parable of Extravagant Love" by Lloyd John Ogilvie from AUTOBIOGRA-PHY OF GOD (Regal Books, a division of Gospel Light Publications, 1979). Used by permission.

"One Solitary Life" author unknown, quoted from MOTIVATION TO LAST A LIFETIME by Ted W. Engstrom (Daybreak Books, 1984).

"Cecil B. De Mille" by Billy Graham. This excerpt was taken from "Christ, the Center of Christmas" (Decision magazine December 1987, © 1987 Billy Graham Evangelistic Association). Used by permission. All rights reserved.

"Object Lesson" by John MacArthur from THE ULTIMATE PRIORITY (Moody Press, 1983). Used by permission.

"Right on Time" by Ron Mehl from SURPRISE ENDINGS (Multnomah Books, a division of Questar Publishers, Inc., 1993). Used by permission.

"Jump" as retold by Tania Gray, copyright 1995. Used by permission. Retold from brief notes in my object lesson file.

"Appointment with Death" by Peter Marshall as retold by Alice Gray. Heard at the funeral of Tom Sweet, 1994.

"Learning 'bout Prayer" by Howard Hendricks from STANDING TOGETHER (Questar Publishers, Inc, Sisters, OR, 1995). Used by permission.

"The Secret of the Gifts" by Paul Flucke, condensed from THE SECRET OF THE GIFTS (InterVarsity Press, 1982). Used by permission of the author.

"Paraclete" by David Seamands from *HEALING FOR DAMAGED EMOTIONS* (Victor Books, 1981). Used by permission.

"Selling Cattle" by Howard Hendricks from *STANDING TOGETHER*. Ibid.

"What If I Get Tired of Being in Heaven?" by Larry Libby from *SOMEDAY HEAVEN* (Gold 'n' Honey Books, a division of Questar Publishers, Inc., 1993). Used by permission. Memo from Alice: This is a beautifully written and illustrated gift book for children that answers their questions on heaven. It is also one of my favorites!

"My Heart, Christ's Home" by Robert Boyd Munger from *WHAT JESUS SAYS* (Fleming H. Revell, a division of Baker Book House, 1955). Used by permission.

"Footprints" by Margaret Fishback Powers. Used by permission.

"The Applause of Heaven" by Max Lucado from *THE APPLAUSE OF HEAVEN* (Word Publishing, Inc. 1990, 1995).

Step 1 God's Purpose: Peace and Life

God loves you and wants you to experience peace and life—abundant and eternal.

The Bible Says . . .

"... we have peace with God through our Lord Jesus Christ." Romans 5:1

"For God so loved the world that He gave His only begotten Son, that whoever believes in Him should not perish but have everlasting life." John 3:16

"... I have come that they may have life, and that they may have it more abundantly." John 10:10b

Since God planned for us to have peace and the abundant life right now, why are most people not having this experience?

Step 2 Our Problem: Separation

God created us in His own image to have an abundant life. He did not make us as robots to automatically love and obey Him, but gave us a will and a freedom of choice.

We chose to disobey God and go our own willful way. We still make this choice today. This results in separation from God.

Our choice results in separation from God.

The Bible Says . . .

"For all have sinned and fall short of the glory of God." Romans 3:23

"For the wages of sin is death, but the gift of God is eternal life in Christ Jesus our Lord." Romans 6:23

Our Attempts

There is only one remedy for this problem of separation.

Through the ages, individuals have tried in many ways to bridge this gap . . . without success . . .

The Bible Says . . .

"There is a way that seems right to man, but in the end it leads to death." Proverbs 14:12

"But your iniquities have separated you from God; and your sins have hidden His face from you, so that He will not hear." Isaiah 59:2

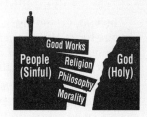

Step 3 ## God's Remedy: The Cross

Jesus Christ is the only answer to this problem. He died on the Cross and rose from the grave, paying the penalty for our sin and bridging the gap between God and people.

The Bible Says . . .

". . . God is on one side and all the people on the other side, and Christ Jesus, Himself man, is between them to bring them together . . ." 1 Timothy 2:5

"For Christ also has suffered once for sins, the just for the unjust, that He might bring us to God . . ." 1 Peter 3:18a

"But God demonstrates His own love for us in this: While we were still sinners, Christ died for us." Romans 5:8

God has provided the only way . . . we must make the choice . . .

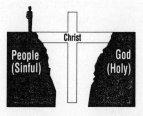

Step 4 Our Response: Receive Christ

We must trust Jesus Christ and receive Him by personal invitation.

The Bible Says . . .

"Behold, I stand at the door and knock. If anyone hears My voice and opens the door, I will come in to him and dine with him, and he with Me." Revelation 3:20

Are you here . . . or here?

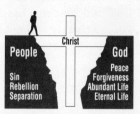

"But as many as received Him, to them He gave the right to become children of God, even to those who believe in His name." John 1:12

". . . if you confess with your mouth the Lord Jesus and believe in your heart that God has raised Him from the dead, you will be saved." Romans 10:9

Is there any good reason why you cannot receive Jesus Christ right now?

How to receive Christ:

1. Admit your need (I am a sinner).
2. Be willing to turn from your sins (repent).
3. Believe that Jesus Christ died for you on the Cross and rose from the grave.
4. Through prayer, invite Jesus Christ to come in and control your life through the Holy Spirit. (Receive Him as Lord and Savior.)

What to Pray:

Dear Lord Jesus,

I know that I am a sinner and need Your forgiveness. I believe that You died for my sins. I want to turn from my sins. I now invite You to come into my heart and life. I want to trust and follow You as Lord and Savior.

In Jesus' name. Amen.

_____   _____
Date   Signature

God's Assurance: His Word

If you prayed this prayer,

The Bible Says...

"For 'whoever calls upon the name of the Lord will be saved.'"
Romans 10:13

Did you sincerely ask Jesus Christ to come into your life? Where is He right now? What has He given you?

"For it is by grace you have been saved, through faith—and this is not from yourselves, it is the gift of God—not by works, so that no one can boast." Ephesians 2:8,9

The Bible Says...

"He who has the Son has life; he who does not have the Son of God does not have life. These things I have written to you who believe in the name of the Son of God, that you may know that you have eternal life, and that you may continue to believe in the name of the Son of God." 1 John 5:12–13, NKJV

Receiving Christ, we are born into God's family through the supernatural work of the Holy Spirit who indwells every believer...this is called regeneration or the "new birth."

This is just the beginning of a wonderful new life in Christ. To deepen this relationship you should:

1. Read your Bible every day to know Christ better.
2. Talk to God in prayer every day.
3. Tell others about Christ.
4. Worship, fellowship, and serve with other Christians in a church where Christ is preached.
5. As Christ's representative in a needy world, demonstrate your new life by your love and concern for others.

God bless you as you do.

Billy Graham

If you want further help in the decision you have made, write to:
Billy Graham Evangelistic Association P.O. Box 779, Minneapolis, Minnesota 55440-0779